Essential
Bali &
Lombok

by Sean Sheehan

PASSPORT BOOKS
NTC/Contemporary Publishing Company

SO-CON-028

Above: Legong *dancer*

Page 1: *rice fields,
Pupuan*

Page 5a: Legong *dancer*
5b: *models of surfboards*

Page 15a: *Uluwatu*
15b: *painting in Ubud's
Museum Neka*

Page 27a: *Gili Trawangan*
27b: *statue in Nusa Dua*

Page 48: *Puri Saren
Agung detail*

Page 66: *rice fields,
Pupuan*

Page 78: *a young Sasak*

Page 91a: *paintings in the
Kerta Gosa, Klungkung*

Page 117a: *Balinese cloth*

Published by Passport Books, an imprint of NTC/
Contemporary Publishing Company, 4255 West Touhy
Avenue, Lincolnwood (Chicago), Illinois 60646–1975 U.S.A.

Copyright © The Automobile Association 1998
Maps © The Automobile Association 1998

The contents of this publication are believed correct at
the time of printing. Nevertheless, the publishers cannot
accept responsibility for errors or omissions, nor for
changes in details given. We are always grateful to
readers who let us know of any errors or omissions
they come across, and future printings will be updated
accordingly.

Published by Passport Books in conjunction with
The Automobile Association of Great Britain.

Written by Sean Sheehan

Library of Congress Catalog Card Number: on file
ISBN 0–8442–0114–6

Color separation: BTB Digital Imaging, Whitchurch,
Hampshire

Printed and bound in Italy by Printer Trento srl

The weather chart on **page 118** of this book is
calibrated in °C. For conversion to °F simply use the
following formula:

$$°F = 1.8 \times °C + 32$$

Contents

About this Book

Essential *Bali and Lombok* is divided into five sections to cover the most important aspects of your visit to Bali and Lombok.

Viewing Bali and Lombok pages 5–14
An introduction to the islands by the author
    Bali and Lombok's Features
    Essence of Bali and Lombok
    The Shaping of Bali and Lombok
    Peace and Quiet
    Bali and Lombok's Famous

Top Ten pages 15–26
The author's choice of the Top Ten places to see in Bali and Lombok, each with practical information.

What to See pages 27–90
The four main areas of Bali and Lombok, each with its own brief introduction and an alphabetical listing of the main attractions
    Practical information
    Snippets of 'Did You Know…' information
    4 suggested walks
    4 suggested tours
    2 features

Where To... pages 91–116
Detailed listings of the best places to eat, stay, shop, take the children and be entertained.

Practical Matters pages 117–24
A highly visual section containing essential travel information.

Maps
All map references are to the individual maps found in the What to See section of this guide.
For example, Gunung Agung has the reference ➕ 29E3 – indicating the page on which the map is located and the grid square in which the mountain is to be found. A list of the maps that have been used in this travel guide can be found in the index.

Prices
Where appropriate, an indication of the cost of an establishment is given by **£** signs:
£££ denotes higher prices, **££** denotes average prices, while **£** denotes lower charges.

Star Ratings
Most of the places described in this book have been given a separate rating:
😊😊😊   Do not miss
😊😊   Highly recommended
😊   Worth seeing

Viewing
Bali &
Lombok

Sean Sheehan's Bali & Lombok

Travelling on *Bemos*

Bemos are minibuses that travel fixed routes and can be flagged down anywhere along their route. They are very common on Bali and Lombok. *Bemos* do not display numbers, destinations or charges and the inexpensive fare is paid direct to the driver or conductor. It is best to have loose change ready and it helps to have some idea of the likely fare by enquiring at your place of accommodation. On Lombok you will also find *cidemos*, two-wheeled horse-drawn carts, that operate in the same manner.

The art galleries in Ubud are a highlight of any visit to Bali

It is not difficult to eulogise Bali and Lombok, even though they are only two of over 17,000 islands that make up Indonesia. Bali is unique, not least because it is the only Hindu society in the whole of southeast Asia. Over a million tourists now pour into the island every year and yet it is still easy to be delighted and intrigued by the Balinese way of life. The people are deeply religious, enormously talented and artistic, and possess a natural grace that will disarm even the most cynical tourist. And, just for good measure, the island is blessed with superb beaches and a permanent summer that endows every day with a glorious abundance of flowers and flowering shrubs, guaranteed to turn any gardener green with envy. Along with the sunshine comes an inexpensive cuisine that is well tuned to Western tastes, one more aspect of a highly creative culture. In case this picture of Bali seems too idyllic to be true, there is also Kuta, a tourist capital relentlessly catering to the materialistic whims of visitors.

To the east of Bali lies the smaller island of Lombok. The people here are mostly Muslims and the feel of the place is quite different; Lombok is a place to retreat to, a place to forget about the Western world. Between them, Bali and Lombok offer an enjoyable and beguiling mix of culture and consumerism, relaxation and escape.

Bali & Lombok's Features

Geography
Bali and Lombok are two of the smaller islands of the Indonesian archipelago that stretches for some 5,000km between Malaysia and Australia. Bali is only 140km from east to west, 80km from north to south, while Lombok is even smaller at 80km by 70km.

Soubriquets
'Morning of the World', 'Land of a Thousand Temples' (20,000 actually), 'The Last Paradise', and 'Island of the Gods' are only some of the soubriquets reflecting the charm of Bali.

Population
Bali has 3 million inhabitants and Lombok has about 2½ million. In July and August Bali's population increases to 4 million due to the massive influx of visitors. Lombok receives 100,000 visitors annually.

Language
Bahasa Indonesia is the national language of Indonesia and is learnt in the schools. The Balinese have their own language and the Sasak inhabitants of Lombok speak Sasak. English is widely understood across Bali, but in Lombok English is spoken in tourist areas only.

Caste
The Balinese language has three forms of address depending on the caste of the person being addressed and the situational context. The choice of a first name for a Balinese child is also governed by caste and there is a surprisingly small number of names available for each caste. Ask a Balinese about this; it is a fascinating topic of conversation.

Religion
The overwhelming majority of Balinese are Hindus and, apart from a small number of people in East Java, are the only Indonesians to follow this religion. Balinese Hinduism is a fusion of mainstream Hinduism with elements of Buddhism and animism. The majority of people in Lombok are Muslims.

Time and effort goes into creating offerings of fruit at a temple

7

Essence of Bali & Lombok

A major attraction is the opportunity to appreciate a living culture that is different and surprising. In Bali, Hinduism is suffused with animism, the belief that the spirit world is everywhere. The countless number of temples, shrines and devout rituals, such as the tiny offerings of flower petals laid on the pavement, are only the outward signs of a spirituality and tranquillity that visitors may grow to envy.

The sun shines almost continuously upon both islands, the stunning beaches are ideal for water sports and the rich culture has produced an astonishing array of arts and crafts for every budget.

THE **10** ESSENTIALS

*If you only have a short time to visit Bali &
Lombok, or would like to get a really complete
picture of the islands, here are the essentials:*

• **See at least one Balinese
dance** (➤ 112) – preferably in
Ubud where there is also a
chance to see a rare all-
women's *gamelan* orchestra.
• **Spend an evening in Kuta**
– love it or hate it, a night of
shopping and entertainment
here is quite different to
anywhere else (➤ 38)!
• **Spend time around Ubud**
– this cultural and artistic
capital (➤ 50–5) is a must for
anyone interested in the arts.
Seek out the paintings,
traditional and modern, in
Ubud's art galleries (➤ 25)
and in Penestanan (➤ 61).

• **Attend a temple festival** –
the tourist board issues a
festival calendar, and visitors
are welcome.
• **Visit a volcano** – there are
plenty of volcanos on the
islands to choose from:
Gunung Agung (➤ 17) and
Gunung Batur (➤ 18–19) in
Bali, Gunung Rinjani (➤ 83) in
Lombok.
• **Watch the sun set over a
temple** – Tanah Lot (➤ 47)
and Uluwatu (➤ 26) are
renowned for their sunsets.
• **Be inspired by the sun
setting over the horizon**
while you stroll along a
tropical beach – Lovina
(➤ 72–3) and the Gili Islands
(➤ 16) are great spots.
• **Worship the sunshine and
acquire a suntan** – but never
forget you are only 143km
south of the equator and the
average temperature is 26°C.
• **Find time to relax and talk
with the Balinese** – ask
about the caste system of
their names or tooth-filling
ceremonies.
• **Try some snorkelling** – it is
easy, safe and utterly
engrossing.

*Images of tranquillity,
secular and religious,
from Bali and Lombok*

9

The Shaping of Bali & Lombok

500,000 BC
During the Ice Ages, when the sea levels are lower, the land masses of Australia and southeast Asia are joined by land across the Indonesian archipelago, allowing the migration of the earliest animals and humans. Bali and Lombok, however, are believed to have remained separated (▶ 84).

300 BC
The Bronze Age sees the development of many of the earliest settlements on Bali, while Lombok remains lost to time. In the coming centuries Indian traders introduce Hinduism to parts of the archipelago.

AD 1343
Bali is colonised by a Hindu kingdom from Java and during the 16th century, when the Javanese empire loses out to Islam, Bali emerges as a place of refuge for Hindu believers. Islam bypasses Bali but not Lombok.

This sculpture from the Museum Bali is inspired by Hindu mythology

1588
The Portuguese plan to erect a fort on Bali to exert command over the important spice islands but their ship sinks offshore and the surviving sailors are not allowed to leave the island. A decade later, the Dutch arrive and this time some of the Dutch sailors voluntarily decide to stay.

1846
The Dutch land their first military force on Bali, followed by another expedition two years later that leads to a fierce battle ending with the Dutch routed by the Balinese. The Europeans return in 1849 and assert their control after a number of bloody battles. The Dutch establish their headquarters in the north of the island but local *rajas* (kings) are allowed to continue their rule.

1891
After 200 years of resisting Balinese incursions, eastern Lombok decisively throws off its Balinese overlords. Lombok, however, is ruled by the Dutch before the end of the century.

1906
The Dutch extend their control to the south of Bali by attacking Denpasar. The Balinese nobility march out defiantly and suicidally to meet the superior military technology of their enemy.

1930s
Tourists begin to arrive on Bali during the 1930s and a small, but significant, number of artists choose to stay.

1941–50
The Japanese invade Indonesia in 1942 and occupy Bali without serious opposition, exposing the Dutch

The Dutch invaded Lombok and Bali, and at Denpasar the Balinese resisted in an act of mass suicide

vulnerability. Within days of Japan's surrender in 1945 Indonesia declares its independence. After four years of fighting the Dutch, independence is gained in 1949. In 1950 a Republic of Indonesia is formed, with Sukarno as president.

1960s
In 1963 Gunung Agung, on Bali, erupts killing and making homeless thousands of Balinese. Further misfortune follows in 1965 when an army officer, Suharto, unleashes anti-communist pogroms that kill thousands more on both Bali and Lombok. In 1968 Suharto becomes Indonesia's second president.

1990s
Bali and Lombok focus on developing tourism as political uncertainties grow within Indonesia over a successor to Suharto.

Peace & Quiet

The Bali Starling

Rothschild's mynah (*Leucopsar rothschildi*), more commonly known as the Bali starling, is now an extremely endangered species. In the mid-1960s it was first classified as in danger of extinction when the total number left in the wild was around 150. Today, there are thought to be only about 50 and breeding programmes are urgently underway to try and preserve the species. The crested bird has bright white feathers contrasting with black wings and a black tip to its tail.

The south of Bali is where most Balinese live and work, and is the region where the majority of visitors stay. Pockets of peace and quiet do exist and in this respect Sanur is preferable to Kuta or Nusa Dua. Candi Dasa, to the east, is a developing resort but it never becomes hectic. Not surprisingly, though, you need to go further afield to feel you are really escaping the crowds. The best balance between tranquillity and visitor comfort lies along the north coast of the island. The beach resort area of Lovina (▶ 72–3) stretches for 8km, and although new accommodation and restaurants continue to open, there is a sense of space and openness about the place that is quite different to the beach resorts in the south. Nightlife is very low-key, with visitors typically spending an evening over a meal, followed by a stroll along the black sand of the beach to watch the sunset. There are no nightclubs or discos. Days are spent relaxing on the beach, snorkelling perhaps, with leisurely visits to places of interest to the west and east of Lovina.

Bali Barat, Taman Nasional

Bali Barat National Park (▶ 56), in the northwest corner of Bali, is rich in wildlife and offers open savannah, long walks and isolation. It is the only place where you might glimpse the Bali starling in the wild, although you are more likely to spot bulbuls, orioles, sunbirds and banded pittas. The Prapat Agung walk is an excellent two-hour trail for bird-watching, while Gunung Klatakan can be climbed in about four hours by anyone seeking strenuous exercise as well as isolation.

Lombok

The island of Lombok offers the most complete escape from the hustle and bustle of towns. Tourist activity is confined to Senggigi (▶ 23) and the Gili Islands (▶ 16), but even these two places are low-key compared with most parts of Bali. The rest of the island is ripe for exploration. With your own transport, seek out deserted beaches, unspoiled stretches of coastline and small traditional villages unused to visitors – the area around Kuta (▶ 84) in the south is particularly good in this respect. For a more active retreat, consider Tetebatu (▶ 90), where the picturesque landscape can be explored on foot.

A peaceful view of Bali through palm trees (left); and the quiet of a deserted Lombok beach (above)

13

Bali & Lombok's Famous

Rice Paddies

One feature of Bali well worth noting is the system of irrigation used to water the terraced rice paddies. The rivers and streams cut too deep into the volcanic rock to allow for easy irrigation, so farmers have cut tunnels through the soft rock and used intricate systems of bamboo pipes to channel the water where it is needed. They are as carefully maintained today as when they were first built – some as long as 1,000 years ago.

Terraced rice paddies are irrigated by elaborate watering systems

The Balinese

It is not world-renowned celebrities that make Bali famous. European artists, who fell in love with the place (and with Balinese women) and stayed, are only famous in their own small way. No, what makes Bali famous is its collective personality – a unique Hindu society in a Muslim nation with a lifestyle and set of attitudes that endears itself to all those who spend time on the island. The Balinese are a genuinely friendly people who have dealt with the annual onslaught of over a million visitors with a degree of success difficult to imagine anywhere else.

Balinese culture expresses itself in a number of ways. Whole villages are dedicated to painting, woodcarving or stonemasonry, and everywhere there is a profusion of natural artistic talent. The performers who faultlessly execute the intricate movements of the famous dances are rarely professionals, and the woman who brings a flask of tea to a guest in her Ubud homestay may well be a player in a *gamelan* orchestra at the weekend.

The Sasaks of Lombok

The Sasaks are the largest ethnic group in Lombok, with their own language and traditions. Unlike the Balinese, but in common with the majority of Indonesians, they are Muslims. Until well into the 1980s most Sasaks had little experience of visitors and even today the majority of islanders' lives are unaffected by tourism.

Top Ten

15

1
Gili Islands

🕂 80A2

✉ Off the northwest coast of Lombok

🍴 Restaurants (£) on all the islands

🚢 From Bangsal throughout the morning; journey time averages 30 minutes

↔ Senggigi (➤ 23), Sira (➤ 88)

These small tropical islands offer seclusion in return for modest tourist facilities. While away the time snorkelling and enjoying the tranquillity.

These three islands – Gili Air, Gili Meno and Gili Trawangan – off the northwest coast of Lombok are becoming increasingly popular with young travellers on a tight budget. The beaches are clean, the coral very accessible, food and accommodation are inexpensive, and nightlife is simple – watching the sunset and socialising over drinks.

Gili Trawangan is the largest, liveliest and most popular of the islands, but it only takes two hours to do a complete circuit of it on foot (➤ 85), and nearly all of the tourist facilities are concentrated along the south coast. Gili Air is

You really can enjoy idyllic solitude on the Gili Islands

❓ **Perama**
✉ Jalan Legian, Kuta, Bali ☎ 0361-751551; and ✉ Padang Tegal, Ubud, Bali ☎ 0361-96316; and
✉ Senggigi, Lombok ☎ 0370-93007
Sunshine tours
✉ Senggigi, Lombok ☎ 0370-93029

the smallest, with hotels and restaurants more evenly spread out, and offers the best balance between the 'party island' atmosphere of Trawangan and the solitude of Gili Meno. Gili Meno has the best accommodation and is the most peaceful of all three islands.

Snorkelling equipment is available for hire on all the Gili Islands, and scuba-diving operators on Air and Trawangan offer PADI (Professional Association of Diving Instructors) courses and facilities for qualified divers. Choose an operator with some care – compare the deals offered and ask other scuba-divers about their experiences.

Most boats leave for the islands from Bangsal. If you are based in Senggigi, consider a day trip direct from Senggigi to Gili Trawangan, organised by Sunshine Tours. The Bali bus company, Perama, runs a bus-and-boat package from places in Bali as well as Lombok. Between May and August try to arrive early in the morning since accommodation is occasionally oversubscribed.

2
Gunung Agung

The highest mountain on Bali (3,142m)
and, with a crater summit over 500m across,
an imposing and unforgettable sight.

The majestic sight of this volcanic mountain dominates the landscape of eastern Bali and both its physical and spiritual presence is keenly felt by the Balinese. In 1963 it erupted with such force that the top 100m were blown into pieces. The catastrophe was widely interpreted as an act of divine displeasure because the mountain has always been revered as the island's most important home for spirits. It is still regarded as the most holy place, as you will soon realise when your guide begins the climb by making an offering at a temple.

Climbing Gunung Agung takes at least five hours from nearby Besakih (the only route that reaches the very summit). Set off in the early hours of the morning in order to reach the top before dawn and before clouds set in.

Take an alternative and easier route from the town of Selat to the south of Besakih. The climb takes about three hours and stops just short of the actual summit, but the views to the east and down into the summit's crater are astonishing. Book guides through the tourist office in Besakih or in the town of Selat (no tourist office), but bring your own supplies, including a torch and some warm clothes. A successful climb does not require any experience of mountain climbing but a guide is required. You do need to be fit as there are steep areas of bare rock. Your efforts will be well rewarded once you reach the top.

29E3

 Bemos run to Besakih from Klungkung and to Selat from Amlapura. Tour buses from Kuta or Ubud

 65km northeast of Denpasar

Bring your own food and water if climbing the mountain

Besakih (▶ 70)

Besakih tourist office is at the car park 🕐 8–6

A guide should be hired (at a moderate cost)

Gunung Agung is the highest mountain on Bali, home to the most important temple, at Besakih, on the island

3

Gunung Batur and Lake Batur

29E3

4km east of Penelokan

Restaurants (£) at Toya Bungkah; Kintamani–Penelokan main road has restaurants (££) along it

Buses run from Penelokan to Denpasar and to Singaraja. *Bemos* run from Penelokan to Songan and Toya Bungkah

Batur caldera: cheap

Penelokan (▶ 73), Pura Ulun Danu Batur (▶ 75), Trunyan (▶ 76)

Lake Batur lies within the crater of Gunung Batur, an active volcano but one which is climbed annually by thousands.

The Batur caldera was created some 30,000 years ago when a huge volcano blew itself to pieces. What remains now is the brooding Gunung Batur and a beautiful crescent-shaped lake. Climbing Gunung Batur (1,717m) is not difficult and there is even a tea shop at the summit. This, and the crowds of people who gather before dawn at the top, make it all seem deceptively normal – until wisps of steam rising from fissures in the rock remind you that this volcano is not extinct.

Scenic Lake Batur, the largest in Bali, is 3km wide and almost three times as long. The lake, revered by the Balinese as home to the goddess Ida Batara Dewi Ulun Danu, is a splendid sight, whether seen from above on the main road or approached on the winding road that twists its way down from Penelokan. About 8km along this road from Penelokan is Toya Bungkah, offering accommodation and a wide range of restaurants. This is also the most straightforward place to begin an ascent of Gunung Batur. The climb takes less than two hours and during the day you don't need to take a guide since the paths are well trodden and easy to follow. The first part of the journey is through a forest, and then it's a climb up the rock face and a scamper

over shifting volcanic sand before a final steep stretch to the top. Consider hiring a guide if you are setting off in early morning darkness to catch the sunrise (a 4AM start is recommended). Ask your guide about having breakfast cooked on the summit.

Nearly all the towns and villages in the vicinity suffer from an over-dependence on tourism. Batur and Kintamani share an interesting temple, Pura Ulun Danu Batur, but little else besides. The lakeside village of Kedisan forms an important junction: bear left for Toya Bungkah, right for the villages of Abang and then Trunyan along the south side of the lake. The stretch of road leading to Abang is particularly picturesque and, though the road ends at Abang, there is a footpath that hugs the lake for a 4km walk to Trunyan. The other road from Kedisan that heads along the north side of the lake takes in the rather decrepit hot springs at Toya Bungkah. Continue on to the quiet village of Songan where there is a restaurant and a temple. Behind this temple a footpath allows a 15-minute walk to a vantage point on the rim of the outer crater. If you have your own transport, explore the road beyond Songan for its solitude and further views of the lake and crater rim.

Gunung Batur and Lake Batur provide a backdrop to a leisurely sale of imitation brand-name watches

4
Gunung Kawi

29E2

North of Tampaksiring, 15km north of Ubud

Daily 7–6

Restaurants (£) in Tampaksiring

Best visited with a tour

Cheap

Tirta Empul (► 64)

Off the main tourist trail, ten 11th-century memorials are cut into the bare rock face at the bottom of a green valley.

There is no definitive interpretation of these 7m-high memorial tombs (*candi*) but the likeliest explanation is that they were sculptured after the demise of an 11th-century king. Archaeologists tend to favour King Anak Wungsu of the Udayana dynasty but no ashes or bones have been found here so they are not burial tombs. Nothing is known of the builder artists, though legend credits the giant Kebo Iwa with the achievement of completing all the memorials in one long night using only his fingernails.

Legend maintains that a royal prince carved these shrines with his fingernails

As you first approach the river four of the *candi* come into view. These are traditionally believed to be dedicated to the king's favourite concubines. The plastered exteriors have worn away, but it is possible to make out the shapes of the false doors that adorned each memorial. On the other side of the River Pakrisan there is a second cluster of five *candi* behind a set of rooms, believed to have been the cells of priests who looked after the site and conducted ceremonies. The five memorials may refer to King Udayana, Queen Mahendradata and their three sons. The tenth memorial is a ten-minute walk away to the south of the four *candi*, back on the other side of the river. It may be a dedication to an important minister or adviser to the royal family.

The road to Gunung Kawi is signposted off to the right on the main road just to the north of Tampaksiring.

5
Lake Bratan

The lake is located in an ancient volcanic crater and there are opportunities for quiet, scenic walks in a cool mountain area.

There are a number of attractions around Lake Bratan that appeal to tourists and Balinese visitors but, as the area is well spread out, it rarely seems crowded. At 1,200m above sea-level, the cool air is ideal for walking and a popular short stroll is from the leisure park at Bedugul (Taman Rekreasi Bedugul) to a group of caves supposedly cleared for the Japanese during World War II. From here an easy-to-follow path leads to the summit of Gunung Catur (2,096m) where there is a small temple. Allow about three hours to ascend. Alternatives include hiring a canoe and paddling around the lake, or playing a round of golf at the nearby Bali Handara Kosaido Country Club, which makes the quite reasonable claim that its fast par-72 course is the only one situated inside a volcanic crater.

Far less strenuous than climbing Gunung Catur is a stroll around the southern side of Lake Buyan, 7km to the north of Lake Bratan. The nearest spot to park is in the village of Yehmas and from here it is easy to walk down to the lakeshore. There is another scenic lake to the west, Lake Tamblingan, best reached by taking the road that heads west from the village of Pucak, which is situated on the main road heading north from Lake Bratan.

29D3

48km north of Denpasar

Bali Handara Kosaido Country Club: 0362-22646

Restaurants (£) in nearby Bedugul

Buses run to Bedugul from Denpasar and Singaraja

Bali Botanical Gardens (► 56), Pura Ulun Danu Bratan (► 63), Taman Rekreasi Bedugul (► 64)

The pagoda-like towers (meru) of Pura Ulun Danu Bratan look down on Lake Bratan

6
Sanur

✚ 29D1

✉ 15km northeast of Kuta

🍴 A full range of
restaurants (£–£££)
along the main road and
in the hotels

🚌 Tourist shuttle buses to
most destinations in
Bali

♿ Few

↔ Museum Le Mayeur
(▶ 39)

*Sanur makes an excellent
base for water-sports
enthusiasts*

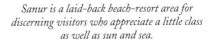

*Sanur is a laid–back beach–resort area for
discerning visitors who appreciate a little class
as well as sun and sea.*

There are three highly-developed beach resort areas in
southern Bali – Kuta, Nusa Dua and Sanur – and Sanur is
for those who wish to escape the excesses of Kuta while
also avoiding the stringently upmarket prices of Nusa Dua.
The beach stretches for about 4km and has the full range
of water sports – snorkelling, surfing, paddle boards,
windsurfing, water-skiing, parasailing – with the better
hotels (▶ 101) having their landscaped grounds and
swimming pools backing down close to the sea. Most of
the hotels are mid-range ones, with a few top notch
names, and a smattering of budget places.

The nightlife in Sanur doesn't pretend to compete with
Kuta but there are plenty of restaurants to suit most tastes
and budgets, a few bars, and a wide range of tourist shops
(▶ 107, 109). The street
hawkers are reasonably
discreet, which contributes to
the general air of relaxation
that characterises Sanur.

For most of this century
Sanur has been tempting
foreigners to settle into
an expatriate life and one
artist's home has become a
museum, the Museum Le
Mayeur. Visitors based in
Sanur will have no problems
though in planning trips
to other parts of Bali. There
are regular tourist buses to
all the popular destinations
and Kuta is close enough to
reach by taxi. For short trips
from one end of Sanur to the
other there are regular
bemos and metered taxis.
Hiring a bicycle is also worth
considering because the
roads are flat and an early
morning cycle ride is a
wonderful way to leave the
beach behind and see the
local farmers busy in their
ricefields.

7
Senggigi

The most developed and enjoyable beach-resort area in Lombok, and the best base for any visit to the island.

The range of accommodation and restaurants, and a laid-back atmosphere, help make Senggigi the ideal place for a relaxing holiday on Lombok. From the airport, in Mataram, or ferry port, at Lembar, it takes little more than half an hour to reach Senggigi's sweeping series of beaches and it is easy to arrange visits and tours to other parts of Lombok from here. There is a direct boat service to Gili Trawangan as well as a Perama tourist bus office with scheduled services to Bali as well as other Lombok locations. Money changers, airline agents, car and bike hire, supermarkets, tourist shops – all thinly spread across Lombok as a whole – are handily located along the one main road that defines Senggigi.

The centre of Senggigi may be taken as the cluster of establishments across the road from the Lombok Intan Laguna hotel (► 103). Five minutes away to the north are shops (► 107) and the Sheraton hotel (► 103), while to the south are more shops and restaurants and the Pura Batu Bolong temple.

Mornings and afternoons are whiled away on the beach or in hotel swimming pools. Evenings are quiet affairs but there are enough decent restaurants to make dinner enjoyable, there are also a couple of pubs, and soothing sunsets can be appreciated from the beach or nearby Pura Batu Bolong.

The road north from Senggigi to Pemenang (22km) follows the coastline and has spectacular views.

It's very easy to find a secluded spot in Lombok – even in the popular resort of Senggigi

80A2

6km north of Ampenan

The widest range of restaurants (£–££) on Lombok

Buses run to and from the ferry port (with onward connections to Bali destinations), airport and other Lombok locations

Few

Gili Islands (► 16), Pura Batu Bolong (► 87), Sira (► 88)

8
Tirtagangga

✚ 29F3

✉ 85km from Denpasar, 20 minutes drive from Candi Dasa

🕐 Water Palace: daily 7–6

🍴 Tirta Ayu restaurant (£) inside the Water Palace grounds (▶ 58)

🚌 *Bemos* to Amlapura from Candi Dasa, then Amlapura to Tirtagangga

✋ Water Palace: cheap

↔ Amlapura (▶ 34), Pura Lempuyang Luhur (▶ 74)

The main attraction is the delightful Water Palace but Tirtagangga also offers cool air, beautiful countryside and opportunities for relaxing walks.

Tirtagangga comes from *Tirta* (holy water) and *Gangga* (from the Ganges) and its Water Palace was built in 1947–8 by the last *raja* of Amlapura. The Water Palace has been damaged more than once as a result of Gunung Agung's eruption in 1963 and an earthquake in 1979. Careful restoration work has preserved the modest grandeur of an elegant channeling system that has water spouting from the mouths of various stone demons into ornamental ponds. Besides admiring the talent of the builders and designers, one can rest in the shade of the garden that is incorporated into the Water Palace, take a plunge into one of the two adjoining pools, or enjoy a drink and the fine view at the Tirta Ayu restaurant that is inside the grounds of the Palace.

The countryside surrounding Tirtagangga is blessed with some of the most impressive rice terraces to be found anywhere in Bali and the reasonably priced accommodation within walking distance of the Palace may tempt you to stay overnight. If so, it is well worth spending a morning walking in the vicinity. With your own transport, an excursion may be made by heading north to the village of Abang, where a sign points to the right for Pura Lempuyang Luhur, 8km away. This temple is perched on top of a mountain and it takes two hours to reach the top, but the view from the temple is ample reward for the effort.

Cooler temperatures around Tirtangangga enhance the charms of its Water Palace

9
Ubud's Art Galleries

An amazing display of indigenous artistic talent, with paintings of all sizes in a variety of styles to suit all budgets.

Do you splash out on a huge canvas of bright green parrots in a tropical setting or opt instead for a detailed Batuan-style miniature where every inch of the canvas is intricately painted? There is more than one traditional style of pictorial painting, in addition to the expressionist work of the Young Artists school and the increasingly popular modernist style that is often abstract in its subject matter. The choice is bewildering and a visit to Ubud's Museum Neka provides an educational introduction to the different styles and themes of Balinese painting; an advisable exercise before visiting some of the countless galleries dotted in and around Ubud. The Puri Lukisan Museum in Ubud, also displays works of art of a high standard. In a short time you will begin to recognise the different themes and styles and notice the qualitative differences between paintings with the same subject. Prices are not always a reliable guide because galleries differ in the percentage difference between their first asking price and the final price they are prepared to settle for; it may range from 15–60 per cent. The best approach is to shop around, practise your bargaining skills, and trust your instincts when choosing a particular painting.

Some of the galleries recommended in this guide (➤ 104) are in central Ubud but quite a few are north of the town centre, on either side of the main road in the vicinity of the Museum Neka. The village of Penestanan, less than an hour's walk from the centre, is an especially delightful place to shop for paintings.

The larger galleries are able to arrange for a framed painting to be shipped home, but an alternative is to dispense with the frame and have the canvas wrapped up inside a sturdy, protective roll.

➕ 52B2

✉ See Paintings, in Shopping (➤ 104)

🕐 Most galleries are open from 8–7 or even later

🍴 Restaurants (£–££) within walking distance of galleries

♿ Few

✋ Galleries: free. Museum Neka: cheap

🔁 Ubud (➤ 50–5), Museum Neka (➤ 51), Puri Lukisan Museum (➤ 53), Penestanan (➤ 61)

A painting by an Ubud artist makes an ideal gift to yourself

10
Uluwatu

A highly revered 11th-century temple perched dramatically on a rock above the crashing waves of the Indian Ocean.

Location – as estate agents proclaim – location, location and nothing can beat the positioning of this most holy temple, balanced on the very edge of a narrow promontory some 70m above the crystal-blue sea and white surf. The actual temple itself would not command anywhere near as much attention if it had been placed inland but its shoreline setting is magnificent. It is best seen at sunset – but this is the time when crowds suddenly appear.

The present temple of Uluwatu was established by a Hindu priest from Jakarta in the 16th century

 29D1

 20km south of Kuta

Restaurants (£) along the road into Uluwatu

Public transport to and from Uluwatu is unreliable; use your own transport or join one of the many available tours

Cheap

Pantai Suluban (➤ 43)

A sash must be worn

The temple is skillfully constructed from coral stone, on arrival, however, your attention is likely to be distracted by the mischievous troupe of resident monkeys. The *candi bentar* (gateway) into the middle area of the temple complex is the only section that can be appreciated at close quarters because the inner part of the temple, that reaches to the cliff edge, is usually closed to visitors. From the outside, though, it is possible to view the three-tiered shrine with its thatched roofs, known as the *meru*. What makes Pura Uluwatu so holy to the Balinese is not aesthetics but its status as one of the island's sacred directional temples dedicated to the spirits of the sea.

To the surfing *cognoscenti* Uluwatu is famous for the surf at nearby Pantai Suluban, accessed by a rough track close to the temple carpark. This beach is unsuitable for swimming but there are a number of inexpensive cafés where you can eat, drink, watch the surfers at play and admire the great ocean view.

What To See

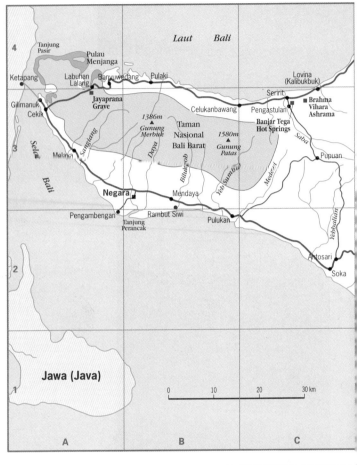

Laut Bali

Tanjung Pasir
Pulau Menjanga
Ketapang
Labuhan Lalang   Banyuwedang   Pulaki
Gilimanuk   **Jayaprana Grave**
Cekik   Celukanbawang   Pengastulan
Melaya   1386m   **Banjar Tega Hot Springs**
                         ▲ Gunung Merbuk   Taman
                                           Nasional   1580m
                           Bilibeob   Bali Barat ▲ Gunung Patas
                                                                      Pupuan
Negara   Mendaya   Yeh Sumbul
Pengambengan   Rambut Siwi   Pulukan
                  Tanjung Perancak
                                                                      Antosari
                                                                      Soka

Selat Bali
Sangiang
Daya
Medewi
Saba
Yebbatian

Seririt
Lovina (Kalibukbuk)
■ Brahma Vihara Ashrama

Jawa (Java)

0   10   20   30 km

A   B   C

1   2   3   4

Most Balinese depend
upon the farming of rice
for their livelihoods

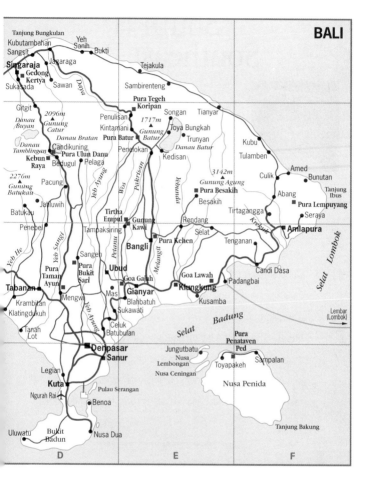

BALI

Tanjung Bungkulan
Kubutambahan
Sangsit
Singaraja Jagaraga
Gedong
Kertya
Sukasada Sawan
Gitgit
Danau 2096m
Buyan Gunung
Catur
Danau Candikuning
Tamblingan Pura Ulun Danu
Kebun Bedugul
Raya
2276m Pacung
Gunung
Batukau Jatiluwih
Batukau
Penebel
Tabanan
Krambitan
Klatingdukuh
Tanah
Lot

Yeh
Sanih Bukti

Tejakula

Sambirenteng

Pura Tegeh
Koripan
Penulisan Songan Tianyar
Kintamani 1717m Toya Bungkah
Pura Batur Gunung
Batur Trunyan
Penelokan *Danau Batur*
Kedisan

Mengwi
Pura Pura
Taman Bukit
Ayun Sari
Mas
Celuk Goa Gajah
Batubulan Gianyar
Blahbatuh
Sukawati

Tampaksiring
Sangeh
Ubud

Tirtha Gunung
Empul Kawi
Bangli
Pura Kehen

3142m
Gunung Agung
Pura Besakih
Besakih

Kubu
Tulamben
Culik Amed
Bunutan
Abang Tanjung
Pura Lempuyang
Tirtagangga Seraya
Amlapura
Rendang
Selat
Tenganan
Candi Dasa

Goa Lawah
Klungkung Padangbai
Kusamba

Lembar
(Lombok)

Selat Badung
Pura
Penataven
Jungutbatu Ped
Nusa Toyapakeh Sampalan
Lembongan
Nusa Ceningan
Nusa Penida

Denpasar
Sanur
Legian
Kuta
Ngurah Rai
Uluwatu Bukit
Badun Nusa Dua
Pulau Serangan
Benoa

Tanjung Bakung

D   E   F

South &
Southeast Bali

The south of Bali is where all visitors to the island first arrive and is where a fair number spend all or most of their time. The airport is here, close to the administrative capital Denpasar and even closer to Kuta and other highly developed beach resort areas. Kuta is Bali's infamous tourist capital, enjoyed and abhorred in equal measure, while the nearby resort of Sanur offers a quieter alternative.

Cultural highlights in the south include the ancient temples of Tanah Lot and Uluwatu, both perched on the shoreline and both attracting hordes of hawkers that come in the wake of tour buses. The southeast of Bali is well worth exploring as an escape from the commercial hustle and bustle that is in danger of swamping parts of the south. A day or two spent in the small resort village of Candi Dasa is a perfect way to unwind and relax.

' If anything, tourism has pumped more life into the Balinese cultural Renaissance that began earlier this century. There are probably more superb artists and craftsmen in Bali today than at any time in its history. '

International Herald Tribune
(1986)

Denpasar

Denpasar is probably one of the least-visited capitals of a major tourist destination but this is partly because the hedonistic allure of Kuta is too strong to compete with and Denpasar has busied itself evolving into a working city in its own right. It has only been called Denpasar since 1949 when newly independent Bali asserted itself by shifting the capital from Singaraja in the north, where the Dutch had based themselves, to Badung in the south which was then renamed Denpasar.

Denpasar translates as 'north of the market' and the market itself is definitely worth experiencing, even if nothing is purchased. The more sedate Museum Bali (▶ 32) that is near by also merits a visit for an introduction to Balinese culture. The best way to enjoy Denpasar is by devoting a morning to walking around it (▶ 37) because this provides an opportunity to see a rare urban aspect to Bali. The city population is fast exceeding 400,000 and the Balinese share their city with an increasing number of Muslims from Java and Lombok, while Chinese immigrants run many of the shops and small businesses. There are plenty of non-tourist shops to browse through.

Public transport connects Denpasar with most corners of Bali but if you are based further south in Kuta, Sanur or Nusa Dua it may be worth travelling to and from Denpasar by taxi as many of the *bemo* stations are spread out around the city perimeter and away from the places of interest. There is little reason to stay overnight in Denpasar and the choice of restaurants is poor so a morning visit is best (Museum Bali is not open in the afternoons).

Umbrellas, used by the Balinese for village events, on sale to tourists in Denpasar

What to See in Denpasar

MUSEUM BALI

This museum was founded by the Dutch in the early decades of this century but it wasn't completed until 1932. There are four sections to the museum, each housed in a separate building, and the main two-story building is the one facing the entrance. The ground floor has archaeological finds while upstairs contains farming equipment and sculptors' tools. The other three buildings contain an eclectic range of exhibits: ceremonial dress and accessories, religious artefacts, a model of a cremation ceremony, textiles, and spinning equipment. The building with the sandstone statues outside has splendid examples of both black and white magic characters from Balinese dances as well as some superb dance masks.

33A2
Jalan Letkol Wisnu, near Puputan Square in the centre of town
Sun–Thu 7–2, Fri 7–11, Sat 7–12.30. Closed: Mon
The nearest restaurant (£) is at the Natour Bali Hotel in Jalan Veteran
Cheap

PASAR BADUNG

The grim exterior of the three-storey building that houses Denpasar's largest market gives little indication of the teeming life inside. The ground floor spills over with every type of fruit and vegetable grown on Bali and visitors are guaranteed to discover at least a dozen unknown examples of local food. The first floor is a warren of small shops dedicated to household goods and dried food, while the top floor is a pot-pourri of textiles, clothing and some handicrafts. Local women tend to persist in offering their service as a guide and firm but polite refusal may be necessary.

33A2
Jalan Gajah Mada
Daily 7–6
Small cafés (£) in the adjoining streets
Tegal bemo station in Jalan Imam Bonjoi serves the southern peninsula, including Kuta and Sanur
Free

PURA JAGATNATA

Next door to the Museum Bali is the modern Pura Jagatnata temple, built in the 1950s though it looks older. All temples have a shrine-tower topped by an empty throne, known as the *padmasana*, and the one here is a particularly fine example made of white coral.

33A2
Jalan Letkol Wisnu
Daily 8–5
Cheap
A sash must be worn

TAMAN BUDAYA CULTURAL CENTRE

The main exhibition here focuses on the history of Balinese painting but this could be skipped if you are planning to visit Ubud's Museum Neka (▶ 51) which presents a more educational overview. Other exhibits are devoted to dance masks, woodcarving and other handicrafts. Traditional dances are performed most nights in the adjoining amphitheatre and, in the summer months, there are often special exhibitions and performances.

33A2
Jalan Nusa Indah
Tue–Sun 8–5. Closed Mon
Small restaurant (£) in the Centre
Kereneng bemo station
Cheap

Museum Bali is a work of art in its own right

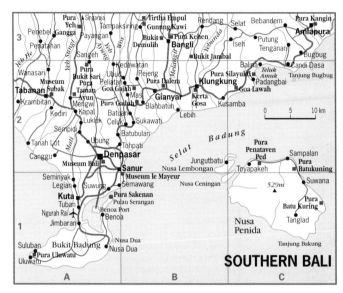

SOUTHERN BALI

33

Ganesh, the elephant god, receives the finishing touches at Batubulan

34

What to See in South & Southeast Bali

AMLAPURA ✪

This is the main town in southeast Bali and during the eruption of Gunung Agung in 1963 the town, then called Karangasem, was cut off by lava flow which flattened parts of the outskirts. The town was renamed so as to help remove any bad karma. The only attraction open for visitors is Puri Agung, one of the town's royal palaces, also known as Puri Kangin. The main structure inside this palace is the Maskerdam (a corruption of Amsterdam) building, named as a tribute to the Dutch who allowed the Karangasem royalty to retain more of their traditional privileges than granted to other Bali kingships. Unfortunately, the palace evokes little of its past splendours.

BATUBULAN ✪✪

This is a regular stop on the Denpasar to Ubud arts-and-crafts trail and the speciality here is stonecarving. The stone carvers work by the side of the road and it is fascinating to watch them chiselling away at huge blocks of stone. Small portable carvings of mythological figures are also on sale. The best place to appreciate examples of larger finished work is in the temple, Pura Puseh, reached by turning right when exiting from the north end of the village. Next to the temple is a dance stage where morning performances of the *Barong and Rangda* dance are held daily (► 112). Evening dances are also performed on a regular basis.

BENOA ✪

Benoa, also known as Tanjung Benoa, is a narrow finger-like peninsula of land that points north from Nusa Dua. It has recently developed as a water-sports playground for Nusa Dua and boats once used for fishing now ferry surfers and snorkellers.

CANDI DASA ✪✪✪

An increasing number of visitors are now spending a part of their time based in Candi (pronounced Chandy) Dasa, preferring it to the brashness of Kuta or the expense of Nusa Dua. Plenty of decent restaurants, a growing number of bars and shops, tourist amenities and a pleasant character to the resort (no pavement hawkers peddling fake watches and the like) make it an enjoyable accommodation centre. It is well-situated for excursions further east and north and the Perama bus company has an office, on the main road in the centre of town (☎ 0363-41114), for booking day trips.

A drawback for some is the absence of a beach (washed away when the reef was used as building material in the 1980s) but this helps to keep the crowds at bay and there is a sandy beach to the east which is within walking distance. Snorkelling and diving operators are easy to find.

✚ 33C2
✉ 69km northeast of Denpasar
🍽 Excellent range of restaurants (£–££) either side of the resort's main road (▶ 92)
🚌 *Bemos* from Denpasar's Batubulan terminal stop at Candi Dasa en route to Amlapura
🔄 Amlapura (▶ 34), Padangbai (▶ 42), Tenganan (▶ 47)

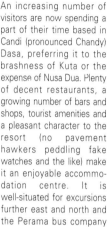

Ornate stone statues, like this one at Candi Dasa, are a typical sight in Bali

CELUK ✪✪

This is the second stop on the Denpasar to Ubud arts-and-crafts trail. Here the exclusive speciality is silverwork: earrings, necklaces, chains, rings, bracelets and brooches. The village is basically a 3km-strip of main road defined by small and large jewellery shops (▶ 105) on both sides. This is a village dedicated to shopping, there are no places to stay and no restaurants. As a general rule, it pays to avoid the grander-looking jewellery shops that provide large parking spaces for tour coaches and seek out instead the smaller establishments.

✚ 33B2
✉ 12km northeast of Denpasar
🚌 *Bemos* running between Denpasar's Batubulan terminal and Ubud stop in Celuk
🔄 Batubulan (▶ 34), Batuan (▶ 57)

GIANYAR ✪

A busy town with an illustrious history but of minimal interest to tourists. There is a variety of temples and a few craft villages dotted around to the west and south but the pretty coastline near the temples is not safe for swimming. Furthermore, despite being famous for *babi guling* (roast pig) there is no tourist-oriented restaurant in the town.

✚ 33B2
✉ 10km southeast of Ubud
🚌 *Bemos* from Denpasar

GOA LAWAH ✪

Goa Lawah, very popular with tours, is a bat cave in a cliff which is also home to a small highly revered temple. Countless thousands of fruit bats inhabit the cave and they will probably be heard and smelled before being seen. Legend tells of a giant snake deep inside the cave which is fed by the bats. An unfortunate aspect of Goa Lawah is the temerity and tenaciousness of the hawkers who will press free gifts on visitors as their opening gambit.

JIMBARAN ✪

This fishing village is south of the airport and boasts an excellent crescent-shaped beach that is never crowded. Tourist developments have been confined to the building of top-class hotels, and visitors without their own transport have little option but to eat in the hotel or take a taxi elsewhere.

KAPAL ✪

This little village is noteworthy for its sculptors and its temple but they are only worth seeing if passing through on a journey (▶ 45). Shops displaying their wares of sculptured figures line both sides of the main road. The temple of Pura Sadat dates back to the 12th century, though the present structure was mostly built in 1949 after being destroyed in an earlier earthquake.

KLUNGKUNG ✪✪✪

The Kerta Gosa at Klungkung ceased to function after the town fell to the Dutch in 1908

The royal palace in the town of Klungkung was home to Bali's most important dynasty until Dutch usurpation in 1908. What remains, inside a landscaped area known as the Taman Gili, is the Kerta Gosa (Hall of Justice) – a legal chamber where participants could gaze at ceiling paintings of wrongdoers being punished by devils and the virtuous enjoying heavenly bliss. The famous paintings that can be gazed at today were completed in the 1940s. Also to be seen is the Bale Kambang (Floating Pavilion), said to be used for royal tooth-filling ceremonies. There is also a small museum which explains the background to the history of Klungkung.

A Walk in Denpasar

This walk begins outside the Bali Natour Hotel.

With the main entrance to the hotel behind you, turn right and walk 100m to the roundabout where Jalan Gajah Mada meets Jalan Surapati. Turn left onto Jalan Surapati until the imposing residence of the governor of Bali is reached, then cross the road to reach the monument and fountain in the park of Puputan Square.

You are following in the footsteps of the last *raja* of Badung and more than a thousand of his people who in 1906 left their palace (now the governor's residence) and committed a ritual suicide (a *puputan*) in the square rather than surrender to the overwhelming Dutch forces.

Walk to the left (eastern) side of the square.

Here Pura Jagatnata (➤ 32) and the Museum Bali (➤ 32) can be visited.

With the museum on your left, walk down to the first junction and turn right, with the south side of the square on your right. Walk straight across the next two junctions onto Jalan Kalimantan.

When walking on Jalan Kalimantan you will pass a good *warung* (a small street-side restaurant ➤ 97) and a traditional perfume shop.

Turn right when you reach a T-junction.

This street, Jalan Sulawesi, has small textile shops.

Cross to the other side of this street before the next crossroads.

Here is the main entrance to the Pasar Badung market (➤ 32). From the market it is a short walk north to the main road, Jalan Gajah Mada.

Turn right onto this busy commercial street that has one souvenir shop on the left side.

Jalan Gajah Mada leads to the roundabout close to the Bali Natour Hotel where the walk began.

Distance
3km

Time
2–5 hours, depending on temple, museum and market visits

Start/end point
Bali Natour Hotel, near Puputan Square
➕ 33A2
🚌 Tegal *bemo* terminal

Lunch
Puri Agung restaurant (££) (➤ 92) in the Bali Natour Hotel
✉ Jalan Veteran
☎ 0361-225681

A monument in Puputan Square pays homage to the heroic victims of resistance to the Dutch in 1906

KUTA ✪✪✪

Kuta is an extraordinary place and no one could have foreseen its development from a 17th-century slave port to an international beach resort pulsating slavishly to the tourist rhythm. A trickle of visitors began in the late 1930s but it wasn't until the 1960s that this started to become a gradual flood. Now, after some 40 years of dedicating itself to tourism, Kuta must have reached its zenith. The thousands of souvenir shops, pubs, restaurants, hotels, boutiques, money-changers and the like have filled every available foot of ground and it is difficult to imagine any further developments.

The neighbouring areas of Tuban, Legian and Seminyak have merged with Kuta to form an 8km stretch, which soon makes walking tiresome. Use the metered taxis when necessary. The main road is Jalan Legian with narrow lanes and smaller streets joining it to the beachside road that runs parallel. In this area, between these roads, lies the heart of Kuta; a few bars in particular attract rowdy groups of young Australians. There are plenty of other pleasant bars and restaurants to enjoy between shopping trips (➤ 105,106,108,109), and Kuta's beach is superb for sunbathing, swimming or surfing.

➕ 33A1

✉ 9km south of Denpasar

🍴 The widest range of restaurants (£–£££) in Bali

🚌 Tourist buses for all destinations can be booked through the Perama office at 16 Jalan Legian (☎ 0361-96316 or 0361-751551))

ℹ The Badung Tourist Office is on Jalan Bakung Sari, (☎ 0361-751419). It is open Mon–Sat 7–5

↔ Sanur (➤ 22), Uluwatu (➤ 26), Denpasar (➤ 31–2), Jimbaran (➤ 36)

Did you know ?

In 1936 an American couple, Bob and Louise Koke, came from California to Kuta and, impressed by the tourist potential of the beautiful beach, decided to build a small hotel which flourished until 1942 when non-paying Japanese guests turned up uninvited. The site of Bali's first hotel is now home to the Natour Kuta Beach Hotel (➤ 101).

MUSEUM LE MAYEUR ✪✪

Adrien Le Mayeur (1880–1958) was a Belgian artist who settled in southern Bali in the 1930s, when he was in his early fifties, and married Ni Polok, a locally famous and stunningly beautiful *legong* dancer who was a teenager at the time. Their new home was built on the beach in Sanur and after Ni Polok's death in 1985 the house became a museum. The paintings on display are not as interesting as the building itself which has been little altered over the years and retains its original carved windows and doors. The museum is at the northern end of Sanur's beachfront (turn right at the bottom of Jalan Hang Tuah).

🚹 33A2
✉ On Sanur's beachfront
🕐 Tue–Thu 8–2, Fri 8–1:30, Sun 8–4. Closed: Sat
🍴 Restaurants (£–££) within walking distance
🚌 Denpasar *bemos* stop nearby on Jalan Hang Tuah
👜 Cheap
↔ Sanur (▶ 22)

NUSA DUA ✪✪

This is a purpose-built upmarket beach resort, on the eastern tip of the Bukit peninsula, made up of internationally famous five-star hotels (▶ 101) rubbing shoulders with one another and nearly all running down to the beach. Nusa Dua is Bali's showcase resort, with its biggest convention centres complementing the exclusive hotels.

🚹 33A1
✉ 25km south of Denpasar
🍴 Many of the best restaurants in Bali (£££)
♿ Few
↔ Uluwatu (▶ 26), Jimbaran (▶ 36)

There is a good beach, though bathers tend to prefer their hotel swimming pools. Guest facilities are second to none and it would be easy to stay here a week or more and never visit the same restaurant or bar a second time. Unfortunately, the only distraction to hotel life is the centrally located Galleria complex (▶ 109) which consists of top-end consumer outlets retailing clothes and brand-name goods, and restaurants which are almost as expensive, but not as good as the ones in the hotels. If you are without your own transport you will have to rely on taxis, the free buses to the Galleria or the hotel shuttle-bus trips to Kuta.

Alone with the surf on the famous Kuta beach

Food & Drink

Meals, in Bali, are international in their variety and, with the exception of five-star hotels, inexpensive. Western favourites like pizza and pasta are ubiquitous and the fast-food franchises have reached Kuta, but it is the fish and Indonesian dishes that will deliver novel and interesting tastes.

Indonesian Cuisine

The seafood can be relied on for its freshness and variety

A typical Indonesian meal will be based around rice, with side dishes of fish, vegetables and meat, and with the flavour mostly provided by chillis, ginger, turmeric and soy sauce. Fresh, local seafood is definitely worth enjoying more than once. Starters and desserts are not common in Indonesian cuisine and versions of Western favourites may disappoint. Balinese dishes can be difficult to find but many of the smarter restaurants now feature some on their menu. *Babi guling* (roast suckling pig) is a favourite at festivals but not easily served up in a restaurant at short notice. Common dishes are *nasi goreng* (vegetables and some meat and/or fish with fried rice) and *nasi campur* (with boiled rice).

Drinking Water
Do not drink tap water and use bottled mineral water even for brushing your teeth. The ice served with drinks in most tourist restaurants should be reliable but there is no way to be sure; take care in smaller establishments, especially in Lombok.

Vegetarian Food

Vegetarians will have no problem finding non-meat dishes. *Gado-gado* (steamed bean sprouts and fresh vegetables laced together with a spicy peanut sauce) is found on every menu and *cap cai* (pronounced chap chai), which is basically stir-fried vegetables, is also very common. It is easy to tire of these though, so look out for tofu-based dishes (pronounced tahu) which are often imaginatively prepared. The few vegetarian restaurants in Kuta and Ubud are well worth seeking out.

Durians

For a food experience that is truly different, try the infamous durian. The custard and almond taste is sheer heaven to durian devotees but most people are repulsed by the extremely pungent smell. Alfred Russel Wallace claimed they were 'worth a voyage to the East to experience'. Most definitely an acquired taste.

Other Tropical Fruits

The tropical fruits available in Bali are delicious and should not be missed when they are in season. The papaya, guava and mango may all be familiar enough, so try the rambutan with red spiky hairs on the outside and a white and juicy fruit inside. Star fruit is readily identified by its shape and the yellower the fruit the sweeter and riper the taste. Mangosteen's purple-brown shell hides a white fleshy fruit inside while the *salak*, known also as the snake fruit, is the strangest-looking of all; peel its scaly brown shell to get at the luscious, segmented fruit inside. The heavyweight of all fruits is the jackfruit, weighing up to 20kg, with a knobbly green skin and a yellow segmented fruit inside.

Jackfruit (top), rambutan (left), durian, bananas, and papaya (above)

Something to Drink?

Bottled soft drinks, coffee (*kopi*) and tea (*teh*) are widely available, though the local coffee is served black and unfiltered. Opinion varies as to the taste quality of local beers (*Bali Hai, Bintang, Anker*) but imported beers are becoming more common and tourist bars will stock imported spirits. The strongest local spirit is *arak* (distilled from rice), best mixed with 7-Up, or try *brem* (a rice wine) or *tuak* (a beer brewed from the sap of palm trees).

NUSA LEMBONGAN

This small island, 4km by 3km, is visited mainly by surfers because of the good breaks, but it is worth making a trip here if you want a lovely beach mostly to yourself. Bring your own snorkel. At low tide it is possible to wade across to Nusa Ceningan, a uninhabited tiny island off the south coast. Basic accommodation and food is available in the village of Jungutbatu on the west coast. There is not enough water to sustain rice growing and the cultivation of seaweed is the main livelihood of the 2,000 inhabitants. Bamboo frames in the water are used to train the seaweed which is then dried and sold as ingredients for cosmetics and food.

➕ 33B2
✉ 20km off the southeast coast
🍴 Restaurants (£) in Jungutbatu
🚌 Catch a boat from Sanur (ticket office at the northern end of Sanur beach, in front of the Ananda Hotel, near the Museum Le Mayeur)
↔ Nusa Penida (➤ 42)
❗ It is usually necessary to stay overnight as boats depart for Sanur each morning. Package trips are available from the ticket office (see above)

Idyllic bungalows for an overnight stay on Nusa Lembongan

NUSA PENIDA

This island, close to Nusa Lembongan, has the interesting temple of Pura Pentaram Ped, a large limestone cave and a beautiful stretch of beach along the north coast. Sampalan is the largest town but the place to head for is Toyapakeh, in the northeast of the island, close to the lovely white beach. The south coast has spectacular scenery but a hired motorbike is necessary and the roads are not well maintained. The Balinese believe Nusa Penida is home to Jero Gede Macaling, a demon whose evil influence needs to be placated through ceremony and prayer.

➕ 33C1
✉ 22km off the southeast coast
🍴 Simple food available in Sampalan (£)
🚌 Boats from Padangbai (➤ 42)
↔ Nusa Lembongan (➤ 42), Pura Penataran Ped (➤ 44)

PADANGBAI

Padangbai, the port for ferry boats to Lombok and tourist trips to Nusa Penida has responded to the tourist trade by developing accommodation and restaurants and is a very pleasant place to stay for a night or two. Snorkelling gear may be hired and there are three temples perched on the eastern headland of the crescent-shaped bay. The most significant of these is Pura Silayukti, reputedly the abode of an important priest in the 11th century.

➕ 33C2
✉ 56km northeast of Denpasar
🍴 Small beach-front seafood restaurants (£)
🚌 Buses to Denpasar and most other destinations
↔ Nusa Lembongan (➤ 42), and Nusa Penida (➤ 42)

Padangbai is the departure point for Lombok – in larger boats than these!

PANTAI SULUBAN ✪

Pantai means beach and Suluban Beach is a famous surfing spot visited religiously by keen surfers drawn by the powerful swell of the breaks. Non-surfers come here to enjoy the atmosphere and relax in the small bars and restaurants that have developed into a mini resort of their own. The beach, which unfortunately is not suitable for swimming, is at the end of a 3km-long track and boys with motorbikes are on hand to taxi people there.

✚ 33A1
✉ 22km south of Kuta
🍴 Small restaurants (£) facing the surf
↔ Uluwatu (► 26)

PULAU SERANGAN ✪

Also known as Turtle Island because of the practice of keeping turtles here until they are weighty enough to slaughter and sell. The island is 3km long and less than half a kilometre wide and, apart from the Pura Sakenan temple which dates back to the 16th century, there is little to see. Notwithstanding the relaxed atmosphere that characterises the island – there are no roads or traffic – a snorkelling trip is the best reason for making a visit to Pulau Serangan.

✚ 33A1
✉ 400m south of Sanur
🍴 Small places serving local seafood (£)
🚌 The easiest way to get here is on a snorkelling trip, readily bookable in Sanur, Nusa Dua or Kuta

PURA DALEM ✪✪

Pura Dalem means Temple of the Dead and every village has one but this Pura Dalem near Gianyar is one of the better examples. It is dedicated to the witch Rangda, who can be seen performing vile deeds in the sculptures near the gate. The tower with the drum bell (the *kulkul* tower), used to summon devotees, is decorated with more unpleasant images of the fate awaiting those sent to hell. There is also a small shrine in front of the temple built in honour of Merajapati, the caretaker of the dead.

✚ 33B2
✉ 3km from Gianyar on the road to Bangli
🕐 Daily 8–4
💷 Free
↔ Bangli (► 56)
❓ A sash must be worn

43

PURA PENATARAN PED

This temple of the dead is on Nusa Penida and is dedicated to Jero Gede Macaling (▶ 42). Its conventional three courtyards are larger than normal because this is an important temple for the Balinese and its anniversary festival attracts a large gathering. The inner courtyard is the most interesting because of its large shrine with skillfully carved doors.

🔲 33C2
📫 5km east of Toyapakeh on Nusa Penida
🕐 Daily 8–6
💷 Cheap
↔ Nusa Lembongan (▶ 42), Nusa Penida (▶ 42)
❓ A sash must be worn

The meru *is one of the most characteristic features of Balinese architecture*

PURA TAMAN AYUN

This large temple, dating back to 1634 and renovated in the 1930s, was the chief place of worship for the Mengwi kingdom until the end of the 19th century. It is now a regular stop on many coach tours. It has an unusually large number of the small multi-tiered shrines (*merus*) that are found in all temples and the inner courtyard has a small moat of its own. The outside of the temple is picturesquely surrounded by another broader moat filled with lotus flowers and lilies. It is thought the palace was designed to model Mount Meru, the mythical home of the Balinese gods that the sea surrounds.

🔲 33A2
📫 Mengwi village, 18km northwest of Denpasar
🕐 Daily 8–6
🍴 The Bali Green restaurant (£) is close to the temple
🚌 *Bemos* from Denpasar to Bedugul stop at Mengwi
💷 Cheap
↔ Tanah Lot (▶ 47), Sangeh Monkey Forest (▶ 63)
❓ A sash must be worn. Outside the temple is a small museum

SANUR (▶ 22, TOP TEN)

South Bali Drive

This drive begins in Kuta, on the main road heading north out of town through Legian and Seminyak. Early in the morning all the traffic will be heading for work in the opposite direction. Other Balinese will already be at work: women on small building sites carrying up to 15 bricks on their heads, watermelons being sold by the side of the road, rice paddies being tended.

Follow the signs for Sempidi and Tabanan.

You will pass through Kapal (► 36) with its roadside shops.

A junction is soon reached where the signs point north for Mengwi and west for Tanah Lot and Gilimanuk.

A diversion could be taken to Mengwi to visit Pura Taman Ayun (► 44) but, if so, return to this junction.

At this junction follow the sign for Tanah Lot. Along this road, approximately 18km from Kuta, a T-junction is reached. A sign points left for Tanah Lot, 10km to the south.

The temple at Tanah Lot (► 47) is on a rocky outcrop out at sea.

Return 10km to the main road where, instead of turning right for Denpasar, carry straight on (passing a bemo *station on the right).*

Distance
40km (including Tanah Lot)

Time
5 hours

Start/end point
Kuta
➕ 33A1

Lunch
Taliwang Bersaudara
restaurant (£)
✉ Tabanan

Did you know ?

*A temple (*Pura*) is conceived as a home for the gods when they are not in heaven and is best visited during its anniversary celebrations (*odalan*) when villagers pull out all the stops in making their temple as dramatic and attractive as possible. The odalan is an open invitation to the gods to pay a visit so that they can be showered with gifts and displays of gratitude. The statues are covered with coloured cloth and women make their ceremonial entrance carrying stupendous pyramids of fruit and flowers on their heads, but still maintaining incredible poise and balance. Temple etiquette demands that all visitors show respect to the gods by wearing a ceremonial sash. These can usually be hired at the temple or purchased from any fabric shop. A sarong may be required at some temples and skimpy clothing is generally discouraged.*

It is 1.5km from the *bemo* station to the Subak Museum (► 46). Look for a red sign on the left at the bottom of a hill for the Taliwang Bersaudara restaurant. (If you find yourself on a dual carriageway, with a model policeman on duty in the centre of the road, you have gone too far.) This restaurant is next to the museum.

From Tabanan retrace the route back to Kuta.

33A2

Up a hillside road at the eastern end of Tabanan

Daily 7–6:30

Taliwang Bersaudara restaurant (£)

Cheap

Pura Taman Ayun (➤ 44), Tabanan (➤ 47), Tanah Lot (➤ 47)

33B2

13km northeast of Denpasar

Craft market: daily 7–6

A couple of local restaurants (£) outside the craft market as well as some catering to coach tours

Bemos from Denpasar to Ubud stop outside the craft market

Batubulan (➤ 34), Celuk (➤ 35), Batuan (➤ 57)

SUBAK MUSEUM

This museum is not on the tourist trail (and is easy to miss, ➤ 45 for road directions) but is well worth a visit for those with an interest in agriculture. Interesting exhibits include an *okdkan* (a wooden box used for farming festivals), the three types of rice ploughs, and fish-catching implements for use in the rice fields. Visitors are so few that the place may well be opened up just for you and the caretaker is happy to explain and describe the exhibits. The Taliwang Bersaudara restaurant is next to the museum.

SUKAWATI ✪✪

This is another stop on the arts-and-crafts trail between Denpasar and Ubud, and the chief attraction is its centrally located craft market. There is a wide choice of fabrics and this is the place to buy a ceremonial sash for temple visits. Also on sale are sarongs, cloth by the metre, light blankets that serve as bedspreads, and a multitude of baskets, wind chimes and temple umbrellas.

From sunrise to sunset the shops of Sukawati beckon

TABANAN ⬤

Tabanan is one of the eight districts of Bali, and is the name of Tabanan district's capital town. There is little of interest in the town itself, apart from the Subak Museum, but with your own transport it is possible to explore the small villages and coastline to the south. If you head west from Tabanan for 3km, on the main road to Negara, you can take the left turning for Krambitan. This little village is home to royal palaces, both of which may be visited. The road continues south to the coast at Dukuh, where there is a lovely black-sand beach and safe swimming.

TANAH LOT ⬤⬤

This temple's location, perched on a rock with waves crashing about it, is beautiful and viewing the multi-tiered shrines against the falling light of approaching sunset is indeed a memorable event. Unfortunately, this is known to every tour operator in Bali so you will not be alone. With your own transport it is worth turning up for sunrise when the dawn colours also lend dramatic splendour to the distinctive silhouette of the temple. When the tide is out it is possible to clamber over the rocks to the temple base itself. A 16th-century Javanese monk, Nirartha, is credited with founding the temple and it is regarded as an especially holy place. Nirartha went on to establish the Uluwatu temple (▶ 26).

TENGANAN ⬤⬤

Tenganan is a Bali Aga village, inhabited by descendants of the original Balinese who predate the arrival of the Javanese Majapahit kingdom in the 14th century. The village, easily visited from nearby Candi Dasa, has 150 families making up a population of 370. Upon reaching the village you will be met by an English-speaking villager who will act as a guide. Not surprisingly, the tour includes opportunities to purchase village-produced items like bamboo calendars, baskets and batik. A special type of cloth (*geringsing*) is woven in the village but it is expensive. During the summer months a number of festivals are held here and the event to try and catch is the *Perang Padan* (held between mid-June and early July) when mock but bloody fights are held using the thorny leaves of the pandanus as weapons.

To arrive at Tenganan follow the road signposted to the village, just west of Candi Dasa. After about 1.5km turn left for another 1.5km. Bicycles may be hired in Candi Dasa.

ULUWATU (▶ 26, TOP TEN)

✚ 33A2
✉ 18km northeast of Denpasar
🍴 Taliwang Bersaurada restaurant (£), next to the Subak Museum
🚌 *Bemos* between Denpasar and Gilimanuk
↔ Pura Taman Ayun (▶ 44), Subak Museum (▶ 46), Tanah Lot (▶ 47)

✚ 33A2
✉ 30km northwest of Denpasar
🕐 Ticket office: 7–6:30; viewing possible any time
🍴 Several places to eat (£–££) in the vicinity
🚌 *Bemos* from Denpasar to Gilimanuk pass through Kediri; then to Tanah Lot
👛 Cheap
↔ Subak Museum (▶ 46), Tabanan (▶ 47)

✚ 33C3
✉ 4km north of Candi Dasa
👛 Cheap (you will be asked to sign the visitors' book and make a donation)
↔ Candi Dasa (▶ 35)

Central & West Bali

This section covers the town of Ubud, the most popular destination outside of southern Bali, as well as some of the least-visited parts of the island. Such is the growing popularity of the Ubud area that an increasing number of visitors choose to base themselves inland in Ubud rather than at the established beach resorts to the south. The arts-and-crafts villages around Ubud offer a pastoral idyll and a rewarding chance for visitors to experience the 'real Bali', a unique balance of beautiful countryside, friendly people, and a fascinating culture that seems to happily absorb tourism rather than be weakened by it.

The western side of Bali, by comparison, is rarely visited because, although there is some spectacular scenery, the population density is low and the tourist infrastructure is thin on the ground.

'In Ubud (heart of Bali heart of the world) the arts have thrived forever and the roots of a foreign community have been feeling their way into this outlandish soil.'

INEZ BARANAY
The Saddest Pleasure (1989)

Ubud

Ubud has the unrivalled claim to be the cultural heart and soul of Bali. Despite the masses of small shops, mostly dedicated to paintings, woodcarvings and other arts and crafts, the place miraculously manages to avoid seeming too commercial. Visitors are amazed by the apparent ease with which local artists produce delightful work, and the surrounding countryside, so amenable to meandering walks, is just one of the many reasons why so many make Ubud their favourite town.

Framed and ready to go at one of Ubud's many art galleries

Ever since the artist Walter Spies came to Ubud in the late 1920s travellers have been following in his footsteps, yet, despite the tremendous increase in numbers, the town retains its charm and rarely disappoints those who stay. The atmosphere is subdued and easygoing and it is not a difficult place in which to relax. Quite apart from the absorbing enjoyment of cultural shopping, Ubud offers the best-value dining opportunities anywhere in Bali. Restaurateurs have responded to the tourist market with the same talent and flair that characterises the work of local artists. The quality of accommodation, in Ubud and in its neighbouring villages, is equally impressive and caters to all budgets.

The original village of Ubud has now grown into a town that includes once-neighbouring villages like Penestanan and Peliatan, but the central crossroads remains the junction where Ubud Palace meets Monkey Forest Road (the tourist information office is here also). The surrounding countryside is easily reached by a short walk or cycle to the west where, uniquely, one may wander through hamlets where the wonders of nature and agriculture compete for your attention with local artists' displays of paintings and other arts.

What to See in Ubud

ANTONIO BLANCO'S HOUSE ✪

Opinions differ as to the worth of a visit to the theatrical home-turned-gallery of the most flamboyant of Ubud's contemporary expatriate artists. His paintings, mostly exotic ones of semi-clad females, adorn the walls and there is no mistaking the artist's personality that impresses itself upon every room.

✚ 52B2
⊠ Off Jalan Raya Campuan
🕐 Daily 7–5
🍴 Restaurants (£–££) within walking distance
✋ Cheap

MONKEY FOREST ✪

The monkeys here are too used to tourists and they can aggressively pester anyone who they think is hiding food. Keep a tight hold on any valuables, as the monkeys are known to grab more than just food. More interesting and less demanding is the Pura Dalem (Temple of the Dead) situated inside the forest. There are restaurants on Monkey Forest road.

✚ 52B2
⊠ At the south end of Monkey Forest Road
🕐 Daily 7–6
🍴 Restaurants (£–££)
✋ Cheap
↔ Nyuhkuning (▶ 60)

MUSEUM NEKA ✪✪✪

This is the best gallery in Bali and should not be missed. The first of the rooms displays examples of the major schools of Balinese art, the earliest being the traditional two-dimensional Kamasan style which gave way in the 1930s to the Ubud style, influenced by Western artists with their notions of perspective and much concerned with the effects of light and shadow. The Batuan style is best represented by *Busy Bali* by Wayan Bendi, packed with dense details (including tourists all with long noses!). A second room is devoted to Bali's best known artist Gusti Nyoman Lempad (▶ 52); his paintings of tales from Indian epics and local folklore are very well explained in the museum, and his *Mother & Father Brayut* series and his *Battle at Langkapura* are deservedly popular. Another room, displaying works from other parts of Indonesia, has the astonishing *Three Masked Dancers* by Anton Kustia Widjaja. The final room, entitled 'East meets West', has the work of foreign artists upstairs and paintings by the famous Javanese artist Affandi downstairs. A bookstore at the museum sells books on Balinese art and culture.

✚ 52B2
⊠ Jalan Raya Campuan
☎ 0361-975074
🕐 Daily 9–5
🍴 Café (£) in grounds

Above: *painting in the Museum Neka*

🚌 Bemos heading west stop outside the museum; hail *bemos* outside to return to the centre of Ubud
✋ Cheap
↔ Penestanan (▶ 61)

NYOMAN LEMPAD'S HOUSE

Bali's best-known artist, Gusti Nyoman Lempad, was born in the village of Gianyar but later moved to Ubud where he lived until his death, in 1978, at the apparent age of 116. He is most famous for his ink drawings on paper and while the Museum Neka (▶ 51) has first-class examples of his talent there is very little on display at his home, which is now open to the public.

🞧 52B2
✉ Off Jalan Raya
🕐 Daily 8–5
🍴 Restaurants nearby (£) on Jalan Raya
🎟 Free

PURA CAMPUAN

This temple, also known as Pura Gunung Lebah, stands at the confluence of two rivers and may be visited as part of an enjoyable walk in the Ubud countryside (▶ 54). The temple was renovated in 1991 and contains more than a dozen small thatched shrines and a large coloured statue of a dancing god. To reach the temple from Antonio Blanco's house (▶ 51), cross the road and take the first turning on the left on the other side of the bridge, on the road back into the centre of Ubud. Soon after turning left, turn left again down the steps at the sign that reads 'Going to the Hill'.

🞧 52B2
✉ Campuan, less than 1km west of town centre
🕐 Open 24 hours daily
🍴 Restaurants close by on the main road
🎟 Free
↔ Penestanan (▶ 61)

Right: *Small thatched shrines at Pura Campuan*

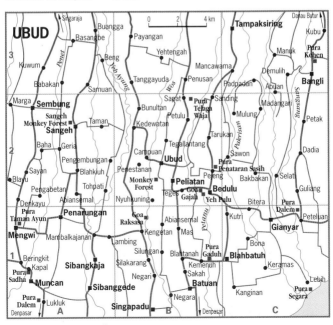

PURA SARASWATI ✪✪

This little temple is famous for its fine examples of Gusti Nyoman Lempad's work (▶ 52). He designed the temple layout and executed the stone carvings that are so attractive a feature of this temple. Especially noteworthy is the rococo lotus-throne shrine upon which photographers practise their close-up techniques. It is upheld as one of Ubud's great examples of artistry. The name of the temple, Saraswati, refers to a revered Hindu river and its associated goddess.

+ 52B2
⊠ Off Jalan Raya, shortly before the Puri Lukistan Museum
⊘ Open 24 hours daily
🍴 Restaurants (£) within walking distance on Jalan Raya
💷 Free

PURI LUKISAN MUSEUM ✪✪

Puri Lukisan, Palace of Fine Arts, has recently been renovated and it now forms a useful complement to the Museum Neka. It was founded in the mid-1950s through the combined efforts of an Ubud prince and the Dutch artist Rudolf Bonnet (1895–1978). These two men had been earlier closely involved in the *Pita Maha* movement which developed as a response to the first wave of tourist interest in Bali. The movement sought to preserve artists' integrity while also integrating it with more Western influences and the success of this venture may be judged by the high standard of much of the work on display in the Puri Lukisan. The gallery is set in lovely grounds with ponds, fountains and gorgeous flowers.

+ 52B2
⊠ Jalan Raya
⊘ Daily 8–5
🍴 Restaurants (£–££) within walking distance on Jalan Raya
💷 Cheap
↔ Penestanan (▶ 61)

A detail from the serene gardens surrounding Puri Lukisan Museum in Ubud

UBUD'S ART GALLERIES (▶ 25, TOP TEN)

A Walk in the Ubud Countryside

Distance
12km (6km if a *bemo* is used to return to Ubud)

Time
4 hours (2 hours if a *bemo* is used to return to Ubud)

Start point
Pura Campuan
➕ 52B2

End point
Lungsiakan village (with the option of continuing to Penestanan)
➕ 52B2
🚐 Any *bemo* travelling in the direction of Ubud

Lunch
Bridge Café (££) (➤ 58). The Bridge Café is 1km after the Hotel Tjampuhan on the main road towards Ubud
✉ Campuan
☎ 0361-975085

This walk begins at Pura Campuan (➤ 52–3).

Behind Pura Campuan take the ascending paved walkway.

You will see thatched hotel bungalows on your right and fields of elephant grass on both sides. Farmers are likely to be seen cutting the grass into bundled stoops for thatching or bringing their ducks to the rice paddies. The ascending path gradually becomes an undulating one and the main road can be glimpsed over to the left.

Shortly after the paved walkway ends, the small Wayan Wijaya painting gallery (➤ 104) is passed and the pathway leads to a village. At the end of this village a café sells ice cream. Carry straight along the pathway to a larger village, at the end of which a junction is reached.

You should now be at the Lumbung Sari gallery.

Instead of carrying straight on (which would lead to Keliki) turn left and follow the pathway which crosses a bridge.

You will pass through the villages of Payogan and Lungsiakan.

The pathway comes out on the main road and the centre of Ubud is 6km away to the left. Any bemo travelling in this direction may be hailed or, if still feeling fit, walk 2km in the direction of Ubud as far as the Hotel Tjampuhan (➤ 102), cross the road and take the small road.

This leads to the delightful village of Penestanan (➤ 61).

'Behind Pura Campuan take the paved walkway...'

PURI SAREN AGUNG ✪✪

More commonly known as Ubud Palace, this building stands at the T-junction formed by Jalan Raya and Monkey Forest Road. Until the 1940s it was home to the local ruling dynasty. The compound is now open to the public who may wander around at will. It is best visited twice: once in daylight, when artistic details can be picked out on the sculptures and woodwork, and then again at night when the interior is dramatically lit for regular dance performances.

🕂 52B2
✉ Jalan Raya, north end of Monkey Forest Road
🕐 Open 24 hours daily
🍴 Ubud's restaurants (£–££) are all around
💷 Free

Bougainvillea at Puri Saren Agung

SENIWATI GALLERY OF ART BY WOMEN ✪

This gallery was established by Mary Northmore, a British expatriate artist, and is dedicated to redressing the male bias that features in most galleries of Balinese art. Some of the work on display is for sale and the Gallery has a small shop around the corner on Jalan Raya retailing other arts and crafts produced by women.

🕂 52B2
✉ Jalan Sriwedari
☎ 0361-975485
🕐 Daily 10–5
🍴 Restaurants (£) on Jalan Raya
💷 Free

WALTER SPIES' HOME ✪

The German artist Walter Spies (1895–1942) settled in Ubud in the late 1920s and built a bungalow-style dwelling with two levels outside the village in Campuhan, overlooking the Wos Barat river. He designed the swimming pool (still in use) and entertained famous guests like Charlie Chaplin, before turning his home into a guest house which later expanded to become the Hotel Tjampuhan (▶ 102). Hotel staff are happy to point out Spies' home, presently the hotel's largest room but one which may eventually be developed into a memorial museum. When making a visit it is worth wandering through the hotel's lovingly landscaped grounds which drop down to the riverside.

🕂 52B2
✉ Hotel Tjampuhan, Jalan Raya Campuan
☎ Hotel: 0361-975368
🍴 There is a restaurant (£) in the hotel (▶ 95)
🔁 Penestanan (▶ 61)

55

What to See in Central & West Bali

BALI BARAT, TAMAN NASIONAL ⊕⊕

Covering over 750sq km, the Bali Barat National Park covers a large portion of the northwestern end of Bali. Entrance to the park is from Cecik. There are a number of walking trails (▶ 13), which can only be undertaken with the help of a park guide, but there are no restaurants or shops within the park so bring your own food and drinks. Another attraction in the National Park is Pulau Menjangan, a tiny uninhabited island off the northern coast. This island is reached by boat (a half an hour journey) from Labhuan Lalang, which is just to the west of Banyuwedang. Bring your own snorkel as the island is deservedly renowned for its coral reefs and the calm sea makes it ideal for beginners.

BALI BOTANICAL GARDENS ✪

Easily located off the main road heading north through Bedugul, the Bali Botanical Gardens (also known as Kebun Raya) were set up in 1959 and have over 600 different species of trees and more than half as many orchids. The large tree at the first roundabout past the entrance is a fine example of a *suku* (podocarp). Unfortunately not everything is labelled in English, but this may improve in time. There is a mosque near the Gardens and Islamic prayer chants are heard through loudspeakers every Friday – an unusual sound in Bali.

BANGLI ⊕⊕

The Bangli kingdom was the last one to come under Dutch control (1909) and visitors come to the town of the same name to see the impressive temple of Pura Kehen,

handsomely laid out on the terraces of a hillside. The temple's bell tower (*kulkul*) is tucked inside a huge banyan tree in the first courtyard. Also worth seeing is Pura Dalem Pengungekan, a typical temple of the dead adorned with illustrations of the divine retribution awaiting sinners in the next world.

Left: *the open-mouthed face of Bhoma repelling evil from the doors of Pura Kehen*

Right: *the entrance to Goa Gajah may represent Rangda, a legendary widow-witch*

BATUAN

This is another village on the Denpasar to Ubud arts-and-crafts trail. It has given its name to a genre of Balinese painting, characterised by tiny figures and a density of detail, begun in the 1930s when village artists started to experiment with a new style. Today, a variety of styles are available and it takes a while to filter out shops retailing tacky reproductions from the genuine artist galleries.

BEDULU

Once upon a time – before the mid-14th century – Bedulu was the capital of a powerful empire. Visitors today tend to just drive through on their way to somewhere else, but its Pura Samuan Tiga (Temple of the Meeting of the Three), just to the east of the village junction, which dates back to the 11th century, is a significant reminder of past glories.

BLAHBATUH

The village of Blahbatuh is famous for its Pura Gaduh temple and in particular a giant carved head that is commonly taken to represent the mythical giant Kebo Iwa. The ancient head is centuries older than the temple itself, which was reconstructed after its destruction in an earthquake in 1917. A sash must be worn.

GOA GAJAH

The 'Elephant Cave' is believed to have been an abode for Hindu and Buddhist priests dating back to the 11th century, but nowadays it mainly attracts coach tours because of its closeness to Ubud and easy accessibility (it is on the main Ubud–Gianyar road). The entrance to the cave, shaped into the giant mouth of a demon, is far more dramatic and interesting than the actual interior.

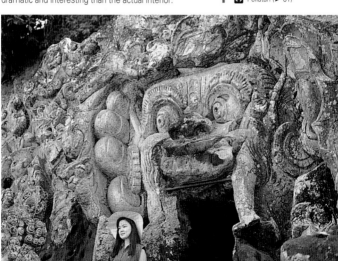

In the Know

If you only have a short time to visit Bali and Lombok, or would like to get a real flavour of the islands, here are some ideas:

10
Ways To Be A Local

Smile graciously, like the Balinese.
Avoid overt shows of emotion in public.
Always wear a sash when entering a temple.
Dress modestly if attending a temple festival.
Use your car horn frequently to alert other road users to your presence.
Be aware of Muslim sensibilities on the island of Lombok.
Do not discuss religion or Indonesian politics unless you know your company.
Haggle over prices but keep a sense of humour.
Use discretion when taking photographs of people, especially at temple festivals.
Accept the fact that notions of punctuality are quite flexible in Bali and Lombok.

10
Good Places To Have Lunch

Bali Aga (£), Lovina Beach (no phone), 1km west of the Playa Beach Hotel on left side of road. Pizza, pasta, seafood and Indonesian dishes.
Biyu-Nasak (£), Lovina Beach (☎ 0362-41176), is Balinese for 'ripe bananas'. Tempting food plus books and magazines

to read, and a children's corner.
Bridge Café (££), Campuan, Ubud (☎ 0361-975085). Try the *blackened ahi* (tuna salad) or *lau-lau* (popular Hawaiian dish).
Café Arma (££), Ubud (☎ 0361-975742), at the southern end of Jalan Hanoman. A lovely open-air location, with rice paddies behind the restaurant, serving Italian food.
Café Dewata (£), Jalan Hanoman, central Ubud (☎ 0361-96076). Perfect for a light lunch after shopping. Try *wrap-wrap* (steamed vegetables, *tempo*, *tahu* and grated coconut).
Café Espresso (££), Senggigi, Lombok (☎ 0370-93148), just south of the Sheraton hotel. Small but quality menu. Games of scrabble and chess available.
Kendedes (£), Padang Bai (☎ 0363-41476), overlooking the ferry port and serving fresh seafood like barracuda and marlin.
Puncak Sari (£), Penelokan (☎ 0366-51073), out of town on the main road to Kintamani. Spectacular views from the outside tables. Lunch buffet and à la carte.
Tirta Ayu (£), Tirtagangga (☎ 0363-21697), inside the Water Palace grounds. Peaceful atmosphere with Indonesian and Western food, including *tahu*

panggang (tofu with chips and salad).
Warung Choice & Bakery (£), 150 Jalan Tamblingan, Sanur (☎ 0361-288401), looks an ordinary place but the food, and desserts in particular, are very good.

10
Top Activities

Bird watching: bring binoculars to Bali Barat National Park and the lakes around Bedugul.
Bungee jumping: take a leap of faith with Bali Bungy Co (☎ 0361-752658) in Kuta. Free transportation within Kuta, Sanur and Nusa Dua area.
Cruising: Bali Hai Cruises (☎ 0361-720331) visit Nusa Lembongan; Spice Cruises (☎ 0361-286283) have three-night adventures to islands east of Lombok.
Diving: Sanur and Candi Dasa in Bali, and Senggigi in Lombok, all have reputable diving operators catering for beginners and professionals.
Golf: Bali Golf & Country Club (☎ 0361-771791) in Nusa Dua or the Bali Handara Kosaido Country Club in Bedugul (► 21).
Snorkelling: plenty of snorkelling spots around the coast, gear usually available for hire.
Surfing: the best breaks are in the south of Bali, from April to October.

Suitable for beginners and experts alike.
Swimming: spoilt for choice as regards beaches but always look for designated swimming areas.
Walking: Long-distance trails in the Bali Barat National Park. Also in the mountains: Gunung Agung and Gunung Batur in Bali, Gunung Rinjani in Lombok.
Water sports: sailing, windsurfing and other watersports are well-organised activities in Kuta, Sanur, Nusa Dua and Benoa.

Learning to jet ski on Lake Bratan

10
Best Buys

'Antique' furniture of all sizes and descriptions, even made to order!
Batik cloth, sold everywhere and versatile in its uses.

A wood carving in the workshop of an Ubud woodcarver

Clothes, there are numerous boutiques and larger stores selling a wide variety of clothes in Kuta.
Fake designer-name watches in Kuta and Senggigi, but do not expect an international guarantee!
Ikat cloth, produced by a special technique.
Inexpensive arts and crafts sold in Senggigi, Lombok (some of the arts and crafts come from islands further to the east).
Jewellery in Kuta, Ubud and Celuk.
Paintings in Ubud. Souvenirs, such as wind chimes and metal candle holders.
Wood carvings sold in the villages around Ubud and Mas.

10
Things To Avoid

Drinking water from taps.
Driving as if in your home country.
Losing your temper or raising your voice, both actions are viewed as uncouth by the Balinese.
Making eye contact with a street vendor if you don't wish to purchase their wares.
Money changers with calculators that work to your disadvantage (always calculate the sums yourself).
Nude bathing, apart from in the beach resorts in south Bali.
Stepping on the little offerings placed by Balinese on the pavement.
Sunbathing without first applying plenty of sun-tan lotion.
Swimming outside designated swimming areas on the beach.
Touching people's heads; this action is offensive to Hindus.

To reach the workshops of this Peliatan woodcarver takes less than half an hour of walking from central Ubud

GUNUNG KAWI (► 20, TOP TEN)

LAKE BRATAN (► 21, TOP TEN)

MAS ✪✪

Long famous as a woodcarving village, most visitors tend to only see the huge mansions of shops that are set in their own grounds on either side of the 5km-stretch of road that runs through Mas. Some of the smaller shops are well worth seeking out. All budgets and tastes are catered for and, while some of the bigger stores have very high-quality products with correspondingly high price-tags, it is still possible to find attractive pieces of art at affordable prices.

MUSEUM PURBAKALA ✪

The archaeological importance of the Pejeng area is considerable (► 61). However, the Museum Purbakala hosts a fairly disappointing collection of finds. Unimpressive examples of Sung- and Yuan-dynasty jars and dishes, and poorly preserved clay stupas from the 8th to 10th centuries, are typical of the artefacts inside the rooms. Outside in the grounds, though, are a group of sarcophagi placed on four sides around a pond and these justify a visit to the museum.

NEGARA ✪

This is the largest town on the west coast and has little to interest visitors except for its annual buffalo racing, which takes place in August and then again around September/October. From Negara the road continues to Gilimanuk at the western tip of Bali but this town, a busy port linking Bali with east Java, has even less to attract visitors.

NYUHKUNING ✪✪

This enchanting village area is well worth a visit for its laid-back atmosphere and scattering of shops selling woodcarvings. Set amidst rice fields to the south of Ubud, it can be found by following the track south from the Pura Dalem in the Monkey Forest. The range is less impressive than that found in Mas but prices are more modest. There is also a small woodcarving museum but wandering into one of the woodcarvers' workshops is a far more absorbing experience.

✚ 52B1
⊠ 4km south of Ubud
🚍 *Bemos* between Denpasar's Batubulan terminal and Ubud pass through Mas and will stop anywhere along the road
↔ Ubud (► 50–5), Peliatan (► 61)

✚ 52B2
⊠ On the right, just after Bedulu, on the road to Tampaksiring
☎ Mon–Thu 7–2, Fri 7–11, Sat 7–12:30
✋ Cheap
↔ Bedulu (► 57), Pura Penataran Sasih (► 62), Pura Pusering Jagat (► 62)

✚ 28B3
⊠ 95km west of Denpasar
🍴 Best place to eat is at the Wira Pada Hotel (£)
🚍 *Bemos* between Denpasar and Gilimanuk stop in Negara
↔ Rambut Siwi (► 63)

✚ 52B2
⊠ 2km south of Ubud
🍴 Pleasant small restaurants (£)
↔ Monkey Forest (► 51)

PEJENG ✪✪

Archaeologists have made important finds in the Pejeng area and the village was once the capital of a kingdom which flourished until the Majapahit invasion in the 14th century. There are three interesting temples, within walking distance of each other, and a small archaeological museum – all are listed in the sidepanel.

PELIATAN ✪✪

Once just a small village famous for its dancers, Peliatan has now merged with the south of Ubud. Jalan Peliatan, the main street in its eastern half, which forms part of the busy route for traffic to and from Denpasar, has the famous Agung Rai art gallery (► 104) and other shops. Apart from shopping, the best reason for being in Peliatan is for a dance performance (► 112), especially one that features the village's all-female gamelan orchestra.

PENESTANAN ✪✪✪

Penestanan has more character and appeal than most of the arts-and-crafts villages in the vicinity of Ubud. It is within walking distance of Ubud (steps and a path almost opposite the Hotel Tjampuhan lead to Penestanan) and is well worth considering as a place to stay for a night or two (► 102). The village was home to a school of Balinese art, the Young Artists of the 1960s, and there are a number of modest galleries (► 104) with examples of this style (and every other style also). With its photogenic scenes of agricultural life and amiable ambiance, Penestanan has managed to retain its rural identity while at the same time catering to the needs of tourists. There are restaurants, craft shops, a money changer and even a reasonably good hairdresser! It is a good place to wander around and relax in.

⊞ 52B2
⊠ 4km east of Ubud
↔ Museum Purbakala (► 60), Pura Kebo Edan (► 62), Pura Penataran Sasih (► 62), Pura Pusering Jagat (► 62)

⊞ 52B2
⊠ 1.5km southeast of Ubud
🍴 A few small eating places (£) along Jalan Peliatan
↔ Ubud (► 50–5)

⊞ 52B2
⊠ Less than 2km west of Ubud
🍴 Pleasant places to eat (£)
↔ Ubud (► 50–5), Walter Spies' Home (► 55)

Gamelan music is played on a variety of bronze percussion instruments, sometimes accompanied by string and wind instruments

52B2
4km northeast of Ubud
Free
Ubud (► 50–5)

PETULU

The attraction here is the splendid sight of countless thousands of white herons and egrets flying in to roost on the branches of trees each evening. It remains a mystery as to why the birds have chosen particular trees in this particular village but they have been doing so for some thirty years. Arrive well before sunset and afterwards stroll beyond the village for scenes of rural bliss as darkness descends.

52B2
In the village of Pejeng
Daily 8–5
Cheap
Museum Purbakala
(► 60), Pejeng (► 61),
Pura Penataran Sasih
(► 62), Pura Pusering
Jagat (► 62)
A sash must be worn

PURA KEBO EDAN

This temple (known also as the Crazy Buffalo temple) has acquired a certain notoriety due to its huge statue of a god or man and his equally huge penis. According to one interpretation the figure boasts six penises, though no one knows quite why, and there is equal uncertainty about the identity of the giant figure itself. To add to the mystery – what exactly is the significance of the apparently female figure that the dancing giant tramples on?

52B2
In the village of Pejeng
Daily 8–5
Cheap
Museum Purbakala
(► 60), Pejeng (► 61),
Pura Kebo Edan (► 62),
Pura Pusering Jagat
(► 62)
A sash must be worn

PURA PENATARAN SASIH

This was the state temple for the Pejeng kingdom but its present claim to fame is to be found inside the inner courtyard. A 3m bronze drum, said to be the largest kettledrum in the world, is at least one thousand years old and carries with it a strange tale. The story goes that it fell from the sky like a fallen moon and landed in a tree. Its brightness hindered the work of thieves, one of whom urinated on it in disgust only to be killed in an ensuing explosion that saw the moon fall to the ground as a drum.

52B2
In the village of Pejeng
Daily 8–5
Cheap
Museum Purbakala
(► 60), Pejeng (► 61),
Pura Kebo Edan (► 62),
Pura Penataran Sasih
(► 62)
A sash must be worn

PURA PUSERING JAGAT

A 14th-century sandstone water-carrier is the attraction at this otherwise standard temple. Balinese couples come here for another reason; the temple is regarded as a source of fertility.

> ## *Did you know ?*
>
> *Balinese temples may seem to come
> in all shapes and sizes but they adhere to a basic plan
> enshrined by tradition.
> There are three courtyards, divided by low walls and
> gateways, with the holiest being the inner one
> that houses the main shrines. All temples have open-sided,
> usually thatched, pavilions (bale) and
> graceful multi-tiered shrines (meru) that always have
> an odd number of levels. The higher the number
> (from three to eleven) the more prestigious is
> the god being honoured.*

The 11-roofed meru of Pura Ulun Danu Bratan is dedicated to Vishnu

PURA ULUN DANU BRATAN ⭐⭐

This scenic temple dates back to 1633, when it was built under the orders of the king of Mengwi and dedicated to Dewi Danu (Goddess of Water). The Balinese consider the lake to be home to the goddess. The temple's striking position, projecting as it does into the lake, almost caused its downfall in the 1970s when the lake water began to rise unexpectedly. The gardens adjoining the temple are very pleasant and ideal for a picnic.

RAMBUT SIWI ⭐

Rambut Siwi is situated about 4km east of Mendaya on the coast road that heads to the west end of Bali. Given its cliff top location overlooking a beach, it should come as no surprise to learn it was founded by the priest Nirartha, who also established Tanah Lot (▶ 47) and Uluwatu (▶ 26). Some of Nirartha's hair is said to reside in one of the shrines in the inner courtyard.

SANGEH MONKEY FOREST ⭐

The forest has a legendary connection with the Hindu epic *Ramayana* for it is said that Rama's general, Hanuman, tried to kill the enemy by dropping a piece of mountain – complete with a band of his monkeys – on them at Sangeh. To say that the monkeys are mischievous is an understatement; watch your belongings. There is a temple, Pura Bukit Sari, in the middle of the forest with an ancient statue of a *garuda* (half-human/half-bird creature from Hindu mythology).

➕ 28D3
✉ Lake Bratan, Bedugul
☎ 0368-21191
🕐 Daily 8–5
🍴 Tourist restaurant (£)
🚌 Cheap
↔ Lake Bratan (▶ 21), Bali Botanical Gardens (▶ 56), Taman Rekreasi Bedugul (▶ 64)

➕ 28B3
✉ 30km west of Soka
🕐 Daily 8–5
 Bemos between Denpasar and Gilimanuk will stop at the turnoff ending at the temple
🚌 Cheap

➕ 52A2
✉ In Sangeh, 21km north of Denpasar
🕐 Daily 8–6
 Bemos run direct to Sangeh from Denpasar
🚌 Cheap

*Bedugal Leisure Park is
on the southern shores of
Lake Bratan*

TAMAN BURUNG

See 'Culture and Wildlife' (► 111) for details of the Bali
Bird Park (Taman Burung).

TAMAN REKREASI BEDUGUL ●

The Bedugul Leisure Park (Taman Rekreasi) is on the right
side of the road as you enter Bedugul from the south. The
quietest activity is to hire a canoe and paddle to the
lakeside temple of Pura Ulun Danu Bratan but there are
also motorised water sports, like jet-skiing, on offer.

TIRTA EMPUL

The holy springs at the Tirta Empul temple have been used
by the Balinese since the 10th century AD. This is not
surprising given the legend that the waters contain the
spirit of immortality after the spring's creation by the god
Indra. The temple and spring complex have been
renovated a number of times and the place is well geared
to receiving Balinese believers as well as tourists. Tirta
Empul is off the main Kintamani–Tampaksiring road, just
north of the turn-off to Gunung Kawi.

YEH PULU ●●●

Although the Yeh Pulu rock carvings lie in close proximity
to Ubud, a surprisingly few number of visitors seek them
out. It is well worth the effort of coming to see the
intriguing and captivating 14th-century figures cut from the
rock face. There may be a narrative link to the panels or
perhaps they are just scenes of everyday life. The second
panel on the left shows an elegant woman alongside a
man carrying wine jars on a pole. The next panel shows a
seated woman alongside a farmer, with other figures to
the sides. Other panels show a hunting group attacking a
boar, and then boars being carried away on a pole. Another
scene shows a woman apparently trying to hold back a
hunter on horseback, or is she being pulled along? Yeh
Pulu can be combined with a trip to nearby Goa Gajah.

A Shopping Drive from Ubud

Depart from Ubud and take the main road south to Denpasar through Peliatan. After about 3km there is a right turn signposted for Denpasar. Ignore this and go straight on.

As well as passing woodcarvers at work by the side of the road, you will come across a large upmarket art gallery, Nyoman Sumerta, and after 1.5km The Duck Man (➤ 107). A little further down this road is the entrance to Goa Gajah (➤ 57). A sign points the way to Yeh Pulu (➤ 64) further along the road.

Carry on for 2.5km and turn right, signposted Denpasar.

You will drive past the village of Kutri and its temple.

Carry on to Blahbatuh (➤ 57) where a diversion can be taken by turning left for Bona.

The shops in the village of Bona are dedicated to bamboo and other woven products: wind chimes, furniture, lampshades, baskets. From Bona return to Blahbatuh.

At Blahbatuh turn right for Denpasar (straight on if returning from Bona) and look for a sign on the left for the Waterfall Restaurant, 1.5km down a side road.

This is a good place for lunch as the view overlooks a waterfall where bungee jumps occur throughout the day.

Once back on the main road it is less than 2km to the next junction. Turn right for Mas (➤ 60) and Ubud.

The first shop worth stopping at, the Pantheon Gallery (➤ 106), is on the left, while further along the road is the smaller but smart Villa Interiors (➤ 106). There are plenty of other shops in Mas to delay your return to Ubud.

Distance
20km

Time
Up to 8 hours, depending on stops

Start/end point
Ubud
➕ 52B2

Lunch
Waterfall Restaurant (££)
✉ Tegenungan, Kemenuh
☎ 0361-299265

The proprietor-to-be of an Ubud craft shop awaits your custom

North & East Bali

The north and east of Bali offers quite a different experience to that provided by the central and southern regions. Although it was in the north that the Dutch established their capital, the area now seems more Balinese and less touristy than the south. This is despite the growing popularity of the Lovina beach area, once a budget traveller's hideout but now catering to everyone while retaining its relaxing and low-key appeal. It is a place where people tend to stay longer than they planned to, deterred from leaving by relatively cheaper expenses and the hospitable nature of a corner of Bali that remains uncrowded. The place that is overrun with visitors, and understandably so, is the volcanic Gunung Batur area in the northeast. A breath-taking caldera with a spectacular lake is one of the most impressive sights anywhere in Bali.

'Lo, from the pasanggrahan we beheld the valley with its blue lake alongside the lava-blackened slopes of the death-dealing volcano, which belched brimstone from its three craters.'

FRANK CLURE
To the Isles of Spice (1940)

Singaraja

The Dutch made Singaraja their headquarters for ruling Bali and the first waves of tourists to the island all disembarked here from their cruise ships. The Japanese also based themselves here during World War II, but after the war the focus shifted to the more heavily populated south. Today, Singaraja is still the largest city outside of Denpasar and, although most visitors tend to pass through it on their way to Lovina, it deserves a closer look.

The tourist office (✉ 0362-61141) is south of town at 23 Jalan Veteran and very close to Gedong Kirtya (➤ 69) and Puri Sinar Nadi Putri (➤ 69). The town's large new temple, Pura Agung Jagatnata, is 2km to the north. It is close to the commercial heart of the city and the main thoroughfare, Jalan Jen Achmad Yani, which runs east–west and out to Lovina. Banks, shops, restaurants and a post office are all located along Jalan Jen Achmad Yani and the old harbour area is just 500m to the north. Singaraja is worth visiting simply for the experience of a Balinese town that is not catering to tourism. At night there is little to detain a visitor except perhaps a stroll around the night market which is located around Jalan Durian, opposite the main junction where Jalan Jen Achmad Yani meets Jalan Gajah Mada.

An arresting view from the Singaraja road

What to See in Singaraja

GEDONG KIRTYA ✪✪
This library has a unique collection of some 3,000 manuscripts inscribed on the leaves of the *lontar* palm. This is the only library of its kind in the world and, though established and maintained for scholars, it is open to the public. The texts are mostly written in Balinese or an old Javanese script and cover subjects like religion, astrology and traditional medicine.

🚩 29D4
✉ 20 Jalan Veteran
🕐 Mon–Thu 8–2, Fri 8–11
Ⓤ Cheap

Patience and skill go into preparing the lontar palms and engraving the text on to them

HARBOUR AND WATERFRONT ✪
The harbour is now little used, with little to suggest its former importance apart from empty warehouses. At the entrance there is an eye-catching monument, built in 1987, commemorating an incident during the struggle for independence in the 1940s when a Balinese was killed by gunfire from a Dutch vessel. There is a small Chinese temple nearby.

🚩 29D4
✉ Jalan Erlangga

PURA AGUNG JAGATNATA ✪
This is a surprising temple simply because it is so new, dating back merely to 1993. It is more likely to be closed than open, but look for the giant elephant-headed figure of Ganesh on the outside of the temple.

🚩 29D4
✉ Jalan Pramuka
🕐 Irregular hours
🍴 Gandi restaurant (£)
    (► 98)

PURI SINAR NADI PUTRI ✪✪
This is a small, inconspicuous weaving factory, easy to miss completely because the entrance is up a lane just to the left of the entrance to the Gedong Kirtya (see above). Visitors are welcome to wander in and are likely to be shown the foot-operated looms clattering and clunking away. All the machines are operated by women and the *ikat* cloth they produce is made by leaving the warp threads (those running lengthwise) undyed while the weft threads (those running across the warp) receive the dye. There is a small room with a modest selection on sale.

🚩 29D4
✉ Jalan Veteran
🕐 Daily 8–4
Ⓤ Free

What to See in North & East Bali

AMED ⭐

Amed is a fairly typical east-coast fishing village which offers spectacular views of Gunung Agung (▶ 17). The black-sand beach is home to a small fleet of local fishing boats and is the workplace for salt-panners.

🕇 29F3
✉ 18km north of Amlapura
↔ Wreck of the *Liberty* (▶ 76)

BANJAR TEGA HOT SPRINGS ⭐⭐

Bring swimming gear and a bar of soap (soap is only allowed in one of the pools) and enjoy a soak in the *air panas* (hot springs). These pools, at Banjar, are well maintained, changing rooms and toilets are provided, and there are a number of small shops close by selling souvenirs, spices (▶ 106), and fabrics. At weekends the hot springs can become crowded but other times you may have the place to yourself.

🕇 28C3
✉ 10km southwest of Lovina
🕐 Daily 8–6
🍴 Komala Tirta restaurant (£)
 Cheap
↔ Brahma Vihara Ashrama (▶ 72)

BESAKIH ⭐⭐

Dramatically situated about 1,000m up the slopes of Gunung Agung, this is the holiest of all temple sites in Bali. The founder is said to be an 8th-century Javanese priest, however the site may well go back to prehistoric times. There are well over 20 temples in all, dominated by the large Pura Penataran Agung, spread out over a length of nearly 3km. Only devotees are allowed to enter the temples but some of the splendour of Pura Penataran Agung may still be appreciated from the outside. Despite the terrifying power of Gunung Agung's eruption in 1963, the Besakih temple complex was not destroyed. Priests are said to have thrown themselves into the flames in acts of desperate appeasement, and most of the post-eruption work involved restoration rather than rebuilding. Try to arrive as early in the morning as possible to beat the crowds.

🕇 28E3
✉ 60km northeast of Denpasar
🕐 Daily 8–5
🍴 Several tourist restaurants (£) outside the complex
🚌 *Bemos* from Klungkung
Cheap
↔ Gunung Agung (▶ 17)

This temple umbrella adorns one of the 22 temples in the Besakih complex

A Countryside Walk

This walk begins just off the main coast road, 10km west of Lovina, where there is a large stone arch across the road that heads inland to Banjar Tega Hot Springs and Brahma Vihara Ashrama. Catch any west-bound *bemo* from Lovina or, with your own transport, park off the main road.

Scenes of rural bliss encountered on a countryside walk west of Lovina

Walk inland for a little less than 1.5km and then turn left at the junction.

At this junction inexpensive rides on the back of a motorbike may be hired as an alternative to a pleasant, though uphill, 7km walk to the next junction.

On arrival at this next junction take the right turn (sign-posted) to the Brahma Vihara Ashrama monastery (▶ 72).

The final 1km walk to the monastery passes through a bougainvillea-lined village with fighting cocks caged in their baskets along the sides of homes. The monastery has a delightful hillside location and there is a small shop close by selling fresh mangoes to quench a thirst.

From the monastery retrace your steps to the junction (8km) where the motorbike rides are hired and turn left. After less than 500m, turn left again for the hot springs (air panas) at the sign-posted junction that points the way.

This stretch of road crosses a small river and passes through a village where there is always something to catch the eye, whether it be children taking the family goat for a walk or baskets of grapes for local wine production. At Banjar Tega Hot Springs(▶ 70) enjoy a bath and a meal.

Finally head back to the main coast road (a walk of 3km).

Distance
8km (16km if a motorbike ride is not hired)

Time
3–4 hours with a motorbike ride

Start/end point
10km west of Lovina on the coast road
✛ 29C3

Lunch
Komala Tirta Restaurant (£)
✉ Banjar Tega Hot Springs

The lotus pond at Brahma Vihara Ashrama is surrounded by 12 statues

BRAHMA VIHARA ASHRAMA ✪✪

This beautiful Buddhist monastery, built in 1972 and repaired after earthquake damage four years later, is unique to Bali and was built with help from Thailand. Just inside the entrance there is a fountain in a lotus pond with 12 statues around it. The whole place has a wonderfully serene atmosphere. As with Hindu temples, it is obligatory to wear a sash and these can be borrowed when making a donation to the monastery.

GUNUNG AGUNG (▶ 17, TOP TEN)

GUNUNG BATUR AND LAKE BATUR (▶ 18–19, TOP TEN)

JAGARAGA ✪✪

The Dutch attacked and took Jagaraga in 1849 and the consequent impact of their colonialism has been famously recorded in the stone of the village's Pura Dalem (Temple of the Dead). The front wall of the temple has an engaging set of panels depicting Balinese life before and after the Dutch. The pre-colonial days are represented by carvings of the climbing of coconut trees and the catching of huge fish, followed by panels showing the Dutch arriving by road and air. On the right side of the entrance the most notable panel is that of two Dutch men in their car being surrounded by Balinese robbers.

LOVINA ✪✪✪

Lovina is the collective name for a beach-resort area strung out along the coast to the west of Singaraja that includes more than one village. Partly because of Lovina's 8km

---

➕ 28C3
✉ 10km southwest of Lovina
🕐 Daily 7–6
👝 Cheap
↔ Banjar Tega Hot Springs (▶ 70)
❓ The monastery may be visited as part of a walk (▶ 71)

➕ 29D4
✉ 9km southeast of Singaraja
🚌 *Bemos* from Singaraja
👝 Free
↔ Pura Bejit Sangsit (▶ 74), Pura Dalem Sangsit (▶ 74), Pura Meduwe Karang (▶ 75)

➕ 28C3
✉ 10km west of Singaraja
🍴 Plenty of restaurants (£–££)

stretch there is little sense of overcrowding but nonetheless the area is growing in popularity all the time. There is an excellent range of restaurants, mostly dotted along the coast road and offering views of unforgettable sunsets from tables close to the beach (▶ 97). Accommodation used to be mainly budget places but more and more mid-range hotels with air-conditioning and swimming pools are opening (▶ 103).

A concentration of visitor facilities have developed around the village of Kalibukbuk, including a small Tourist Information office, money changers and places to hire cars, motorbikes and bicycles. The black-sand beach of Lovina is generally safe for swimming and while it is possible to snorkel directly off the beach, it is equally easy to arrange trips by boat. Diving is possible for both beginners and those already qualified but there is no scope for surfing. Dolphin watching is another favourite activity, beginning around 6AM when you board a *prahu* (traditional Indonesian boat with bamboo stabilizers). Nightlife is fairly quiet, though pubs and bars are springing up and some restaurants offer a dance show or video film.

- *Bemos* from Singaraja
- Banjar Tega Hot Springs (▶ 70), Brahma Vihara Ashrama (▶ 72)
- A tourist office shares premises with the police station in Kalibukibuk, open: Mon–Thu 7–5, Fri 7–1, Sat 7–5

The sunset as seen from Lovina

PENELOKAN ✪✪
The word *penelokan* means 'place to look' and the village has grown on the strength of its ability to offer unparalleled views of a stupendous landscape. Lake Batur, with Gunung Batur on one side and the smaller Gunung Abang on the other, looks truly majestic on a clear day. The only drawback is the location's popularity and the inevitable hordes of hawkers.

- 29E3
- 60km north of Denpasar
- Tourist restaurants (£–££)
- *Bemos* running between Denpasar and Kintamani stop in Penelokan

PUPUAN ✪
Visitors to Pupuan are invariably passing through on their way to or from Seririt on the north coast. The road is a winding and demanding route across mountains, so everyone except the driver enjoys the magnificent scenery all around. At Pupuan there is a waterfall but the real appeal is the views of the surrounding valleys and hills.

- 28C3
- 42km southwest of Singaraja

A detail from a carving in pink sandstone in Pura Beji Sangsit

PURA BEJI SANGSIT ⓒⓒ

It is easy to miss this temple (look for a black-and-blue sign on the north side of the coastal road about 8km east of Singaraja) but it is worth seeking out for the lively energy of its carvings. The exterior panels display some brilliant examples of *nagas* (snake-like creatures) while the gateways into the middle and inner courtyards have a rich profusion of other mythical creatures. As it is dedicated to agricultural spirits, this is known as a *subak* temple. A *subak* is an association of rice farmers sharing a water supply and working together to irrigate their land.

PURA DALEM SANGSIT ⓒⓒ

This temple of the dead can be seen from the road in front of Pura Beji Sangsit and it is reached by threading one's way along the paths between the intervening rice fields and jumping over the occasional water channel. The far left corner of the front wall of the temple has a carved scene of sexual bliss, while the wall to the right of the entrance depicts the horrors of hell. There are other grotesque stone creatures inside the temple and fun can be had trying to determine the nature of some of the pictorial carvings.

PURA LEMPUYANG LUHUR ⓒ

Visiting this temple is very good exercise as it takes about two hours to climb up to it through the forested side of a mountain; the route is signposted from the village of Abang. Upon reaching the summit of Gunung Lempuyang the temple itself may prove to be a little anticlimactic but there is ample compensation afforded by the panoramic view of Gunung Agung. There are places to rest along the route to the top but bring plenty of water and something to eat.

PURA MEDUWE KARANG ✪✪✪

Just past the turn-off for the Kintamani road on the coastal road, 12km east from Singaraja, this is another temple dedicated to the gods of agriculture but, unlike Pura Beji Sangsit, it concerns itself only with dry crops. Many visitors come here to see one particularly famous and much-photographed panel carving, that of a man on a bicycle with flower petal wheels (one of which is about to run over a rat) being pursued by a dog. It can be found at the bottom of the main block in the inner courtyard and it is thought possible that the man, who doesn't look Balinese, is the Dutch artist Nieuwenkamp who travelled around by bicycle in the first decade of this century.

✚ 29D4
✉ 12km east of Singaraja, in the village of Kubutambahan
🕐 Daily 8–5
🚌 Bemos run east along the coast road from Singaraja
💷 Cheap
↔ Jagaraga (► 72), Pura Beji Sangsit (► 74), Pura Dalem Sangsit (► 74)
❓ A sash must be worn

PURA ULUN DANU BATUR ✪✪

An eruption of Gunung Batur in 1926 destroyed the village of Batur and its temple. The community responded by moving up to the crater rim and rebuilding their village and the temple. The temple's importance is reflected in the fact that the *meru* (multi-roofed shrine) has eleven roofed sections, the highest possible number. The temple is also unusual in having extra courtyards adjoining the three conventional ones. The extra space is needed for the annual *odalan* festival (► 116). Most unusual of all, the temple is served by young males selected by a priestess. The senior male priest has an ambassadorial role for the goddess of the lake to whom the temple is dedicated.

✚ 29E3
✉ 2km south of Kintamani
🕐 Daily 8–5
🚌 *Bemos* to or from Singaraja
💷 Cheap
↔ Gunung Batur and Lake Batur (► 18–19), Penelokan (► 73)
❓ A sash must be worn

TIRTAGANGGA (► 24, TOP TEN)

The carvings of Pura Meduwe Karang are a highlight of any visit to the north of Bali

75

29E3
East side of Lake Batur
Boats depart regularly from Kedisan between 8AM and 4PM. The boat ride is 1 hour each way
Boat ride: moderate
Gunung Batur and Lake Batur (► 18–19)

TRUNYAN

The village of Trunyan is inhabited by the Bali Aga, the original Balinese, whose culture predates the Majapahit takeover of the 14th century. There is a footpath from Abang to the village or you may prefer to go by boat from Kedisan. A little beyond the village is the Trunyan cemetery at Kuban, famous because the villagers do not bury or cremate their dead but expose them to the air where the bodies decompose over time. The recently dead are covered up by what is effectively a bamboo coffin. The cemetery is only accessible by boat from Kedisan and many visitors find the whole experience to be a tourist trap.

29F3
35m off the beach at Tulamben, 27km north of Amlapura
Modest choice of restaurants (£)
Bemos from Amlapura and Singaraja
Amed (► 70)

The wreck of the Liberty *is only about 30m offshore and more than 50 divers visit it daily*

WRECK OF THE *LIBERTY*

The *Liberty* was a US cargo ship that survived World War I only to be badly damaged by Japanese torpedoes in 1942 and consequently beached off the eastern coast of Bali near Tulamben village. The eruption of Gunung Agung in 1963 caused the ship to break up and sink into deeper water, and the wreck is now a very popular diving site. It is close enough to the beach to be reached by snorkellers who can glimpse some of the colourful fish inhabiting the coral-encrusted wreck.

29D4
15km east of Singaraja
Bemos along coast road
Daily 7–7
At Puri Sanih hotel (£)
Springs: cheap
Pura Beji Sangsit (► 74), Pura Dalem Sangsit (► 74), Pura Meduwe Karang (► 75)

YEH SANIH

Yeh Sanih, also known as Air Sanih, is a modest beach resort to the east of Singaraja on Bali's relatively untouched northern coast. Its attractions are cold fresh-water springs very close to the sea, but set in landscaped grounds with their own changing rooms. There is a small hotel and restaurant next door. Yeh Sanih makes a pleasant overnight stop while exploring the coastline and there is a temple, Pura Taman Manik Mas, 7km further east along the main road.

A Drive from Singaraja to Lake Batur

This drive begins in Singaraja and finishes in Penelokan.

Start from Singaraja and drive eastwards along the coastal road. After 8km a faded black-and-blue sign on the left of the road points to Pura Beji Sangsit (▶ 74). Drive 200m down the indicated sideroad.

After visiting Pura Beji Sangsit, it is a short walk to Pura Dalem Sangsit (▶ 74).

Return to the main road and continue east for 600m. Look for a sign pointing inland to Jagaraga. (Do not take the narrow lane on the right which the sign seems to be pointing to; the actual turning is 100m further along the road.)

Drive south to Jagaraga (▶ 72). The village's main attraction is the Pura Dalem (Temple of the Dead) with curious facade bas-reliefs depicting Dutch colonists, aeroplanes, cars and bicycles. After your visit, return once again to the main coastal road.

Continue east along the coastal road for 4km, until reaching the junction at Kubutambahan.

Just beyond this junction, on the coast road, Pura Meduwe Karang (▶ 75) may be visited and Yeh Sanih (▶ 76) beyond that.

At Kubutambahan take the inland road south to Kintamani.

About 7km before Kintamani, you will pass Pura Tegeh Koripan temple, and 2km after Kintamani is Pura Ulun Danu Batur (▶ 75). From here it is not far to Penelokan (▶ 73) and the panoramic views of Lake Batur and Gunung Batur.

Distance
42km

Time
5–7 hours, depending on places visited

Start point
Singaraja
✚ 29D4

End point
Penelokan
✚ 29E3

Lunch
Puncak Sari (£) (▶ 98)
✉ Just over 2km before Penelokan on the left side of road
☎ 0366-51073

Penelokan, which translates as 'place to look' deserves its name with views like this of Lake Batur

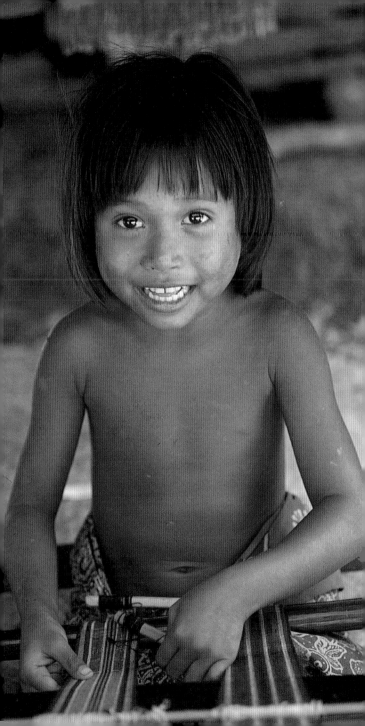

Lombok

Lombok is not Bali. Only 35km separate the two islands but they differ in a number of important respects. The further east one travels in Lombok the more noticeable the different physical landscape becomes. The land is dry and bush-like, with corn and sago often grown instead of rice. Only the north of Lombok has the lushness of Bali, hence the saying 'you can see Bali in Lombok, but not Lombok in Bali'. The indigenous people, the Sasaks, are Muslims and only in the more-developed tourist locations are they becoming as familiarised to visitors as the Balinese. This, of course, is part of Lombok's appeal. The island receives only 100,000 visitors a year and, although there are ambitious plans to develop the tourist infrastructure, Lombok still feels like an unexplored island.

'The remarkable change ... at the Straits of Lombock (sic), separating the island of that name from Bali; and which is at once so large in amount and of so fundamental a character as to form an important feature in the zoological geography of our globe.'

The Malay Archipelago (1869)

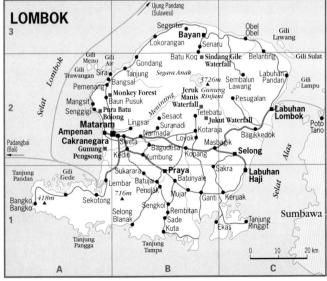

LOMBOK

Ujung Pandang
(Sulawesi)

3

Segenter

Bayan

Obel
Obel

Gili
Lawang

Lokorangan

Senaru

Gili Sulat

Gili
Meno

Gili
Air

Gondang

Batu Koq

**Sindang Gile
Waterfall**

Belanting

Gili
Trawangan

Sira

Tanjung

Segara Anak

3726m

Sembalun
Lawang

Labuhan
Pandan

Gili
Lampu

Pemenang

Bangsal

*Gunung
Rinjani*

Monkey Forest

Jeruk
Manis

Pesugalan

Mangsit

Baun Pusuk

Sesaot

Tetebatu

**Labuhan
Lombok**

Senggigi

**Pura Batu
Bolong**

Lingsar

Suranadi

Jukut Waterfall

Poto
Tano

Mataram

Narmada

Kotaraja

Bagikkedok

Selat Lombok

Ampenan

Sweta

Loyok

Masbagik

Cakranegara

Bagudesa

Kopang

Selong

*Gunung
Pengsong*

Kediti

Kumbung

Selat Alas

Padangbai
(Bali)

Sukarara

Sakra

**Labuhan
Haji**

Tanjung
Pandan

Gili
Gede

Lembar

Batujai

Praya

Batunyale

Ganti

Keruak

418m

716m

Penujak

Mujar

Bangko
Bangko

Sekotong

Sengkol

Rembitan

Ekas

Tanjung
Ringgit

Selong
Blanak

Sade

Sumbawa

Kuta

Tanjung
Pangga

Tanjung
Tampa

0   10   20 km

A   **B**   **C**

Ampenan-Mataram-Cakranegara-Sweta

Not so much the main city on Lombok as a sprawling conurbation spreading eastwards for 8km, engulfing four once-separate towns. One main road, with multiple changes of name, connects the four towns and regular *bemos* shuttle between them. Although the airport and the port are close by many visitors only skirt the towns.

The main tourist office for Lombok (🔲 Mon–Thu 7–3, possibly opening on Fridays in the future. Closed Sat–Sun ☎ 0370-31730) is at 70 Jalan Langko at the eastern end of Ampenan. Ampenan has the island's museum and a Balinese temple, and Jalan Yos Sudarso has shops selling arts-and-crafts from islands to the east of Lombok. Mataram is an administrative centre with little appeal for visitors, but Cakranegara was the island's capital when Balinese influence was at its height in the 18th century and a water palace and a temple remain as a legacy of that era. Cakranegara is also a good place to find somewhere to eat and the top floor of the Mataram Plaza on Jalan Pejanggik has a number of inexpensive food outlets. The town of Sweta forms the eastern end of the conurbation and functions as Lombok's transport capital. Close to the busy bus station there is a large covered market area that is worth a visit.

Ampenan may seen hectic and urban but quiet spots are not difficult to find (left)

Horse-drawn carts, called cidemos, *may be hired for short journeys in Lombok (below)*

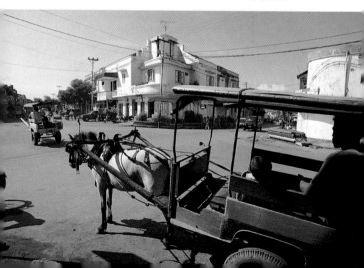

Most of Mayura Water Palace was destroyed by the Dutch in 1894

What to See in Ampenan-Mataram-Cakranegara-Sweta

MAYURA WATER PALACE ✪✪

Built in the mid-18th century, Mayura Water Palace (less well known as Puri Mayura) was the seat of power for the Balinese kingdom that ruled western Lombok at that time. Its appearance may surprise visitors as this 'palace' consists of an artificial lake set in an attractive park, with a raised path leading to a pavilion in the middle of the lake. This pavilion was where justice was meted out under the Balinese kingdom.

PURA MERU ✪

This early 18th-century temple is the largest in Lombok and was built for Prince Anak Agung Made Karang – more for political than religious reasons – in an attempt to unite the various Hindu groups on the island. After entering, turn left to reach the inner courtyard and its three *meru* (multi-roofed shrines). They represent three mountains: Bromo in Java, Rinjani in Lombok and Agung in Bali.

PURA SEGARA ✪

This red-and-white Balinese temple is close to the beach north of Ampenan. It is usually locked but just to the northeast is an old Chinese cemetery that is worth wandering over to. The dirt-track approach road passes through a small settlement which is a sad reminder of the poverty in which many islanders live.

WEST NUSA TENGGARA PROVINCIAL MUSEUM ✪✪

This makes a useful introduction to some aspects of Lombok life. There are paintings of traditional dress and lifestyle, various objects and artefacts from working life, ceramics, musical instruments, shadow puppets, krises (Indonesian daggers with wavy blades), and displays on flora and fauna. A museum guidebook is available in English.

✚ 80A2
✉ Jalan Selaparang, Cakranegara
🕐 Daily 8–4:30 ⚑ Cheap
↔ Pura Meru (▶ 82)

✚ 80A2
✉ Off Jalan Selaparang, Cakranegara
🕐 Daily 8–5
⚑ Cheap
↔ Mayura Water Palace (▶ 82)
❓ A sash must be worn

✚ 80A2
✉ Off Jalan Saleh Sunkar, Ampenan
🕐 Irregular hours, often locked
↔ West Nusa Tenggara Provincial Museum (▶ 82)

✚ 80A2
✉ Jalan Panji Tilar Negara, Ampenan
☎ 0370-32159
🕐 Tue–Sun 8–3
↔ Pura Segara (▶ 82)
⚑ Cheap

What to See in Lombok

BAYAN ✪

The mosque in this small Sasak village on the north coast is regarded as Lombok's oldest, dating back over 300 years, and Bayan may have been the first village to convert to Islam. Ironically, the village is also the birthplace of a Muslim schism, the Wetu Telu religion.

🚹 80B3
✉ 60km northeast of Ampenan
🚌 Bemos from Sweta
🔁 Segenter (▶ 88), Senaru (▶ 88)

GILI ISLANDS (▶ 16, TOP TEN)

GUNUNG PENGSONG ✪✪

It takes half an hour of climbing steep steps (from the temple complex at the bottom) to reach the top of Gunung Pengsong, but the reward is a rich panoramic view of the surrounding countryside, the sea and Gunung Rinjani (▶ 83) in the distance. It helps to set off early in the morning, before clouds set in, to catch sight of Gunung Agung (▶ 17) in Bali. An important harvest festival takes place each year around April. At the summit there is a small Hindu shrine.

🚹 80A2
✉ 6km south of Mataram
🔁 Ampenan-Mataram-Cakranegara-Sweta (▶ 81)

GUNUNG RINJANI ✪✪✪

This is the highest mountain in Lombok (3,726m), the third highest in Indonesia, and is still an active volcano. The mountain is revered by both Sasaks and Balinese, and full moon brings them to the crater rim or the lake to pray and make offerings. During an annual *Pakelem* ceremony, a traditional practice is to throw gifts of gold jewellery into the lake. Climbing to the crater rim (2,634m) from Senaru is easier than aiming to reach the summit as a guide is not required, but a tent and sleeping bag are essential as the climb still requires an overnight stay. The reward is a view of the stunning colours of Segara Anak (Child of the Sea) Lake, and the temptation to spend another day descending to the lake and bathing in the hot springs.

🚹 80B2
✉ 30km west of Senggigi
🍴 Bring your own food and drink
🚌 Bemos from Sweta to Bayan, then take a *bemo* to Senaru

Fine views of Lombok countryside from the summit of Gunung Pengsong

One day Kuta beach in Lombok may be as popular as Bali's beach of the same name

KUTA

Not to be confused with Bali's famous Kuta beach, Lombok's beach is developing as a new resort area along the island's southern coast. The tourist infrastructure is modest but that will all change in time. For the moment, however, Kuta is a quiet, peaceful retreat set amidst stunning coastal scenery. Legend has it that a local princess drowned herself here after being forced to choose a husband and an annual mid-February festival commemorates the event. Within walking distance to the east, the deserted beaches of Seger and Aan beckon but take your own food and water as there are no facilities there.

LABUHAN LOMBOK ✪✪

This is the ferry port for the sparsely populated island of Sumbawa but there is nothing else to attract the visitor. The surrounding countryside is parched and arid, but from Labuhan Pandan, 10km to the north, snorkelling and fishing trips to offshore islands can be arranged.

LEMBAR ✪

This is the ferry port for Bali but visitors who are whisked away on buses to Senggigi or elsewhere miss little. The nearby southwest peninsula is undeveloped but worth exploring with your own transport, preferably a jeep. The road through the peninsula runs through Sekotong and Pelangan before coming to an end at Bangko Bangko, but along the way there are fishing villages where boats can be chartered for visits to small offshore islands. This is relatively unexplored territory and visitors need their own provisions.

Did you know ?

Alfred Russel Wallace (1823–1913) proposed the idea of an evolutionary distinction between Asia and Australia. His division – the Wallace Line – occurred between Bali and Lombok because he believed that the immense depth of the water (1,300m) prevented species from migrating even when ocean levels fell during the Ice Ages. Today, however, scientists believe the differences in flora and fauna are accounted for by different climatic conditions.

A Walk on Gili Trawangan

Gili Trawangan (► 16) lies off the northwest coast of Lombok and a boat trip to the island only takes about 30 minutes.

This is a circular walk around the island, beginning at the point where you land after getting your feet wet disembarking. Turn to your left and head south, following the shore.

You will pass various stalls renting snorkelling gear and, on your right, a small shopping complex next to the popular Restoran Borobudur. Another 1km of walking takes you past the heart of the island's accommodation and there are numerous opportunities to stop and rest for a drink at any of the small restaurants.

The buildings gradually thin out as the southern end of the island is reached and the Sunset restaurant is one of the last places to be passed. On your right, the island's hill (100m) can be climbed as an excursion by taking one of the inland trails, and there are impressive views of Gunung Rinjani (► 83) and Gunung Agung (► 17) from the top. This hilltop is a popular place for watching the ocean sunset.

The entire stretch of pathway that runs along the west side of the island is devoid of buildings. The soil is thin and little can be seen growing apart from coconut trees, cacti and the occasional spread of eucalyptus. A small number of belled cattle and the odd goat may be encountered but that is likely to be all. As the path reaches the north of the island a trail heads inland passing a lighthouse beacon, but carry straight on. Shortly you will find tourist bungalows and restaurants reappearing.

From this point it is less than 1km to the disembarkation point where the walk began.

Boats depart regularly from Bangsal and Senggigi to the unspoiled Gili Islands

Distance
5km

Time
2 hours

Start/end point
Boat harbour (on eastern side of the island)
🚏 80A2

Lunch
Restoran Borobudur (£)
(► 99)
✉ Just south of the start and end point

80B2

15km east of Ampenan

Pura Lingsar: open 24 hours daily

Bemo to Narmada from Sweta, then change for Lingsar

Pura Lingsar: cheap

Narmada (▶ 86)

A floral offering is placed on the head of a demon-guard in Pura Lingsar

80B2

45km east of Ampenan

There is no regular *bemo* service to Loyok. Use your own transport

Tetebatu (▶ 90)

80B2

10km east of Ampenan

Narmada Park: open daily 6–6

Bemos from Sweta

Narmuda Park: cheap

Lingsar (▶ 86), Suranadi (▶ 90)

LINGSAR

The Wetu Telu temple, also known as Pura Lingsar, is the main attraction in Lingsar. It was first built in 1714, rebuilt in 1878, and is unusual for its mixture of Hindu and Muslim Sasak devotees. The two religions have their own compounds, on different levels, and the Sasak

worshippers are members of a minority Muslim sect, the Wetu Telu. The higher courtyard is the Hindu place of worship while the lower one with its own pond is the Wetu Telu area. The pond is alive with eels and devotees have a habit of feeding them with hard-boiled eggs. Usually there are guides waiting outside to show you around but their knowledge may be limited.

LOYOK

This little village's shops are noted for bamboo handicrafts. The bamboo table lamps and wall lamps are some of the better items on sale, but it is worth looking into more than one shop before making a purchase. The nearby village of Kotoraja (Town of Kings), 5km to the north on the road to Tetebatu, has a smaller selection of shops but is more notable for its blacksmithing tradition. Kotoraja was once a place of refuge for Lombok's rulers, hence its name.

NARMADA

Narmada Park (Taman Narmada) was built in 1805 for King Anak Gede Karangasem of Mataram. It is claimed that the gardens, named after a sacred river in India, were designed to model Gunung Rinjani because the king was too frail to climb the real mountain. Apart from the main pond, supposed to model Rinjani's crater lake, Segara Anak (▶ 83), there is a pool open to the public for swimming. At weekends and holidays the park tends to fill up with daytrippers from the capital but when empty it is a pleasant spot to rest and relax in. There is a Balinese temple, Pura Kalasa, in the grounds and the remains of an aqueduct constructed by the Dutch next to the lake, a reminder of Lombok's colonial past.

The garden of Narmada (right) deserves more time than most organised trips allow

PRAYA

The busy town of Praya is the hub for a number of craft villages in the surrounding area. Some 4km to the west is Sukarara village, noted for the quality of its weaving and a favourite stop with tour buses. Most of Sukarara's shops (▶ 108) have large displays, some have their own workshops, and material can be purchased by the metre. The village of Penujak, 6km to the southwest of Praya on the road to Kuta, is noted for its pottery (▶ 106) and watching the potters at work is one of the attractions. The finished products come in all shapes and sizes; unfortunately, a lot of it presents a luggage problem.

🛈 80B1
✉ 25km southeast of Ampenan
🚌 *Bemos* travel between Sweta and Praya

PURA BATU BOLONG

This Balinese temple in the Senggigi area is positioned on a rocky promontory, a natural hole in this rock accounts for the name Batu Bolong (Hollow Rock). Architecturally, the temple is unimpressive but there are excellent views across the Lombok Strait and visitors like to arrive in the evening to watch the sun setting over Bali.

🛈 80A2
✉ 2km south of Senggigi
🕐 Open 24 hours daily
🎟 Free
↔ Senggigi (▶ 23)

SADE

This traditional Sasak village is well prepared for tourists and there is no escaping the company of a self-appointed young guide. Obligatory sights are the rice store, where only women are allowed to enter, and the clay made with the help of buffalo dung that keeps mosquitoes at bay. Sade is a tourist trap but, being on the main road, it is an easy stop for tour buses heading to Kuta. The village has no admission charge, but a small donation is expected when signing the visitors' book. Rembitan village, a little to the north, is much the same but does have an old mosque, closed on Mondays.

🛈 80B1
✉ 3km north of Kuta
🕐 Visit between 8–6
🍴 Closest restaurants are in Kuta (£)
🚌 *Bemos* from Praya to Kuta (some direct from Sweta) stop at Sade
🎟 Cheap
↔ Kuta (▶ 84)

SEGENTER

80B3

2km south of the coast road, signposted between Lokorangan and Bayan

Daily 8–6

Cheap

Senaru (► 88)

Beyond Bangsal, the coastal road that follows the shoreline around the north of Lombok is not often travelled by visitors, other than to reach Senaru for an ascent of Gunung Rinjani. Yet the traditional village of Segenter is worth a visit and is far less of a tourist trap than Sade in the south (► 87). There is no admission charge but visitors are expected to make a small donation when signing the visitors' book.

SENARU

80B3

7km inland from Bayan

Cheap

Gunung Rinjani (► 83), Segenter (► 88)

Senaru is usually only visited by those setting off for a climb up Gunung Rinjani, but this small Sasak village has its own intrinsic interest. The villagers' lifestyle has been little affected by tourism and any opportunity to watch the farmers at work in their fields is rewarding. There is no admission charge but a donation is expected when you are asked to sign the visitors' book.

SENGGIGI (► 23, TOP TEN)

SESAOT

80B2

5km north of Suranadi

Narmada (► 86), Suranadi (► 90)

The white-sand beach at Sira has a remarkable pristine beauty

This little village is easily reached from Suranadi if you have your own transport. The journey is a rewarding one, travelling past villagers laundering in the river and with great views of Gunung Rinjani ahead of you. At the village a rickety bridge, barely navigable by car, leads into a forest with pleasant swimming and picnic spots. A 3km stroll further up the road leads to a smaller village which is also beside the river. Bring your own food and drinks for a picnic.

SIRA

80A2

2km north of Pemenang

Gili Islands (► 16)

This is one of those places that will be unrecognisable in ten years. This tiny village boasts one of the most beautiful beaches in Lombok, a glorious stretch of unbroken white sand looking across to the Gili Islands. Plans are afoot to build hotels and develop a tourist infrastructure but for now there is nothing here but sea, sand and palm trees.

A Drive into the Heart of Lombok

The drive begins in the Ampenan–Mataram–Cakranegara–Sweta conurbation.

The bus and *bemo* terminal in Sweta makes a useful starting point, as it is located on the main road that heads east.

Head east on the road signposted for Narmada (6km).

The park at Narmada (▶ 86) makes a pleasant first stop but consider a short diversion (7km) to Suranadi (▶ 90) for refreshments at the Suranadi Hotel. The signposted road to Suranadi is a left turn at Narmada.

From Narmada, continue east on the main road for 25km and take a poorly signposted (white on a blue background) turning on the left for Tetebatu.

This road first passes the craft villages of Loyok (▶ 86) and Kotaraja before heading north for Tetebatu (▶ 90). There are a number of tourist restaurants either side of the road approaching Tetebatu as well as one in the village itself.

From Tetebatu, return to the main road (11km) that links the east and west of Lombok and turn right (west). You can either return to Sweta or retrace part of the journey as far as the village of Kopang (9km) and turn left to Praya.

From Praya (▶ 87) the pottery village of Penujak and the weaving village of Sukarara may be visited.

Finally, return to Praya and turn left for Mataram.

After 19km the village of Kediri is reached and, if time allows, a diversion could be made from here to Gunung Pengsong (▶ 83) on the west coast.

Otherwise, follow the signs for the main road back to Mataram and Sweta where the journey began.

Distance
83km (excluding diversions to Suranadi or Praya)

Time
6–8 hours

Start/end point
Sweta
✚ 80B2

Lunch
Soedjono Hotel (£) (▶ 99)
✉ Tetebatu
☎ 0370-22159

SURANADI

The holy temple of Suranadi is positioned close to a number of springs, which helps explain why it is named after a heavenly river in Hindu cosmology. The temple itself is unremarkable but the surroundings are pleasing. The nearby Suranadi Hotel was built by the Dutch administration and, although it is architecturally dull, it still evokes a sense of the past and a bonus is its spring-water swimming pool which is open to non-residents for a small charge.

TETEBATU

Tetebatu is the name of a small village on the slopes of Gunung Rinjani. Lacking an obvious focus, such as a temple, it is the scenic and unspoilt countryside that creates Tetebatu's appeal. It is not a place to just visit and leave within an hour; the pleasure comes from strolling through the maze of trails that link the paddy fields. The splendid Jukut waterfall is a 6km walk to the east but shorter walks are also possible. Alternatively you can hire a guide and embark upon a longer excursion. As with other locations in Lombok, the signs of a future tourist industry are plain to see, but for the moment this is still virgin territory. There is a reasonable choice of restaurants; the dining room of the colonial Soedjono Hotel has picturesque views.

80B2
7km north of Narmada
Set meals (££) and à la carte (£) in the Suranadi Hotel
Temple: free
Narmada (▶ 86), Sesaot (▶ 88)

80B2
11km north of the main east–west road
Various places (£) before reaching the Soedjono Hotel

Sasak children at Tetebatu gladly help their parents at harvest time

Where To...

South & Southeast Bali

Prices
Prices are approximate, based on a three-course meal for one person:

£ = under Rp18,000
££ = Rp18,000–30,000
£££ = over Rp30,000

Bukit Peninsula

The Ocean (£££)
On the centre of the Bukit peninsula's southern coast, perched on the side of a cliff 15m above the Indian Ocean. Tables for two under the moonlight with a sea breeze.
📺 **Bali Cliff Hotel, Ungasan** ☎ 0361-771992 🕐 11–10:30

Candi Dasa

Chez Lily (££)
An imaginative menu with a mix of Indonesian and European food. Far more interesting than some of its neighbours offering inauthentic Indian and Italian meals. Videos shown at 7:30PM.
✉ **East end of the main street in town** 🕐 10–10

Kububali (£££)
One of the smartest places to eat in Candi Dasa. An open kitchen, mostly seafood, and the best drinks menu in town.
✉ **The main street in town** ☎ 0363-41532 🕐 8–10

Taj Mahal/Hawaii (££)
A restaurant with a split personality? Suitably eclectic menu of Indian, European and Chinese dishes.
✉ **The main street in town** ☎ 0363-41138 🕐 9–10

Denpasar

Puri Agung (££)
European and Indonesian food best enjoyed amid the faded splendour of the hotel's main restaurant. Alternatively, there is a poolside eating area.
✉ **Natour Bali Hotel, Jalan Veteran** ☎ 0361-225681 🕐 7–10

Kuta

Aromas Café (££)
The best vegetarian restaurant, with blackboard specials and à la carte. Irresistible desserts. Try for a table at the back as the front area is brightly lit.
✉ **340 Jalan Legian** ☎ 0361-751003 🕐 10–10

Bali Asi (£)
Just past TJs restaurant, this is a good-value, informal eatery popular with Australians. A huge menu, and pizza specials between noon and 5PM.
✉ **Poppies 1** 🕐 7:30–10

Bali Aussie Bar & Restaurant (££)
No mistaking the clientele of this popular little roadside restaurant where the atmosphere is more important than the food.
✉ **69 Jalan Melasti** ☎ 0361-751910 🕐 8–11

Bali Satu (£)
This is a small place near the tourist office serving inexpensive seafood and grills. Drinks happy hour is 5:45PM to 9PM.
✉ **Jalan Buri Sari** ☎ 0361-757374 🕐 8:30–11

Golden Lotus (££–£££)
Perhaps the best Chinese cuisine in Bali, the Szechuan dishes will not disappoint.
✉ **Bali Dynasty Hotel** ☎ 0361-752403 🕐 12–2, 6–10

Kempu Café (£)
Simple but filling food in a bamboo-built café: rye bread, toasted sandwiches, lots of fruit drinks.
✉ **Halfway down Poppies**

Lane 1, on the left coming from
Jalan Legian ☎ 0361-751855
🕐 7–10

Mandarin Restaurant (££)
Cantonese, Szechuan and
seafood for lunch and dinner.
Live music in the evening.
✉ **Jalan Kartika Plaza, Tuban**
☎ 0361-751369 🕐 11–3, 6–11

Mini Restaurant (£)
A large restaurant that might
be better named as the Maxi
– or perhaps it refers to the
prices. Good-value seafood
meals.
✉ **36 Jalan Legian** ☎ 0361-
751651 🕐 9–11

Nagasari Restaurant &
Bar (£)
A colourful and popular place
in the heart of Kuta that has
free pick-up-and-return
transportation from local
hotels. Happy hour is
between 4 and 8PM. Regional
and European food.
✉ **Jalan Bakunggari** ☎ 0361-
75188 🕐 9–11

Poppies (££)
A pleasant garden setting of
pools and waterfalls
surrounded by flowers. Make
a reservation because this
place is very popular.
Seafood, regional and
Western dishes.
✉ **Poppies 1** ☎ 0361-751059
🕐 8–11

Taj (£)
An Indian restaurant
overlooking a Kuta shopping
street. Food is not especially
authentic but it makes a
change. Live music.
✉ **Jalan Bakung Sari** ☎
0361-753025 🕐 10–10

TJs (££)
This haven of tranquillity is
tucked away down a lane
running off the southern end
of Jalan Legian. Mexican
food.
✉ **Poppies 1** ☎ 0361-751093
🕐 8:30–11

Legian-
Seminyak

Bali Bungy Co (££)
Dine here as a bungee
jumping spectator not as a
gourmet. Restaurant and bar
(free drink for leapers).
✉ **Jalan Pura Puseh**
☎ 0361-752658 🕐 8–12AM

Kura Kura (£££)
Gourmet dining in this
prestigious restaurant at The
Oberoi. Specialties include
grilled Canadian scallops,
charcoal-grilled tuna steak
and lobster.
✉ **The Oberoi, Legian Beach**
☎ 0361-751061 🕐 6–10

O Pica Pica (££)
Spanish restaurant serving
tapas, paella, steaks and
seafood. Very Spanish and
very touristy.
✉ **7 Jalan Dhyana Pura,
Seminyak** ☎ 0361-730485
🕐 8–12AM

Taj Mahal (££)
Not particularly authentic but
recognisable Indian fare of
curries, naan and tandoori
dishes, best enjoyed in a
small group. Wednesday is
party night.
✉ **Jalan Oberoi, Seminyak**
☎ 0361-730525 🕐 6–12AM

Yanies (££)
Well-established restaurant
and bar specialising in steaks
and hamburgers, but with
plenty of other choices.
✉ **Jalan Tunjung Mekar,
Legian** ☎ 0361-751292
🕐 11–2AM

Nusa Dua

Brasserie des Celebrites
(£££)
Informal dining, reserve a
table with a garden or sea
view. This is a new restaurant,
promising both 'bush tucker'
and health-conscious food.
✉ **Hotel Nikko Bali** ☎ 0361-
773377 🕐 7–10

Ristaffeal
The culinary masterpiece
of Indonesian cuisine is
the *ristaffeal* (from Dutch,
meaning 'rice table'). The
food was originally
prepared by different
households to feed
returning soldiers and it
should consist of at least
ten dishes, usually
including shrimp crackers,
hot chili *sambal* paste,
bean curd, spicy beef,
chicken and duck – all
served with yellow rice
flavoured with coconut
milk.

Balinese Desserts
Western desserts are
often disappointing so try
some of the Indonesian
ones made from sticky or
glutinous rice, like *ketan*
(sugary rice pudding with
coconut milk) or *lemper*
(fruit pudding, with the
emphasis on pudding).
Look out too for durian-
flavoured ice cream and
luridly coloured sweets
made from cassava.

Lagoona (£££)
Seafood and continental
dishes, theme nights, strolling
musicians. Try local seafood
like *bawal* or *baronang*.
✉ **Bali Hilton Hotel** ☎ 0361-
771102 🕒 6–11

Hamabe (£££)
Authentic Japanese cuisine, in
an elegant environment overlooking a Japanese garden.
Shabu-shabu, *teppanyaki*,
sukiyaki and à la carte.
✉ **Sheraton Nusa Indah Hotel**
☎ 0361-71906 🕒 6–11

Makuwa Pakuwa (££)
A new seafood open-air
restaurant in the Galleria
complex. Free shuttle service.
✉ **Galleria Nusa Dua Shopping
Complex** ☎ 0361-772252
🕒 11:30–11

Poco Loco (££)
Mexican food with live music
and a good drinks list. Free
transport within Nusa Dua.
✉ **Jalan Pantai Mengiat**
☎ 0361-773923 🕒 6–12AM

Sateria (££–£££)
Salads, steaks, pizzas, grills.
Beachside location, ideal for
lunch or dinner. Mostly
seafood in the evening,
sometimes theme nights.
✉ **Melici Bali Hotel** ☎ 0361-
771510 🕒 10–11

**The Terrace and The
Restaurant (£££)**
Two restaurants at the
Amanusa hotel offering Bali's
best in sophisticated fine
dining. The Terrace overlooks
a golf course and features
European, Thai and Indonesian
specialties. The Restaurant
has the better wine list.
✉ **Amanusa** ☎ 0361-772333
🕒 11–2, 6–10

Sanur

Agung Bar & Restaurant (££)
Small but tasty selection of
European and local dishes,
plus cocktails. Music on

Tuesday and Friday. Close to
Bali Hyatt hotel.
✉ **97 Jalan Danau Tamblingan**
☎ 0361-288029 🕒 8–10

Choice (££)
The place looks like another
budget, bamboo-and-cane
café but the food is very
good. Chocolate and carrot
cake from its bakery.
✉ **Jalan Danau Tamblingan**
☎ 0361-288401 🕒 7:30–9:30

La Taverna (££)
Beach-side restaurant with
excellent pizzas cooked over
a wood fire. Indonesian
favourites also available.
✉ **La Taverna Bali Hotel, Jalan
Danau Tamblingan** ☎ 0361-
288497 🕒 7–11

Laba-Laba (£)
Large menu, cosy during the
evening, floor show on
Monday and Friday.
✉ **134 Jalan Danau
Tamblingan** ☎ 0361-288132
🕒 8–9

Sita (££)
Seafood and Indonesian
food, nightly performances
of traditional dances. Too
touristy for some, so come
with the right attitude. Free
transport.
✉ **Jalan Ngurah Rai/By Pass
No 41** ☎ 0361-288468 🕒 7–10

Swastika Garden (££)
Attractive garden setting
with choice of Indonesian,
Chinese, seafood and pasta.
Traditional dances on
Thursday and Sunday.
✉ **Jalan Danau Tamblingan**
☎ 0361-288573 🕒 6–10

Telaga Naga (£££)
Across the road from the Bali
Hyatt, this upmarket Chinese
restaurant serves spicy
Szechuan favourites and stir-
fried Cantonese dishes.
Thatched-grass roof
surrounded by lotus ponds.
✉ **Jalan Danau Tamblingan**
☎ 0361-288271 🕒 6:30–10

Central & West Bali

Ubud and Surrounding Area

Ary's Warung (££)
International and oriental food served in a relaxed setting with live music. The food is very good and the atmosphere aims to be cultured. Come here for the whole evening.

✉ Jalan Raya ☎ 0361-975053 🕐 9–1AM

Bumbu (££)
Balinese, Indian, and vegetarian food in the heart of Ubud, opposite Puri Saren Agung (➤ 55).

✉ 1 Jalan Sueta ☎ 0361-974217 🕐 8:30–10

Café Lotus (££)
Quality Asian food, as well as pasta dishes, served at this famous Ubud restaurant, named after a large lotus pond that it overlooks.

✉ Jalan Raya ☎ 0361-975231 🕐 8–10

Café Wayan (££)
One of the best restaurants (see sidepanel), with a dining area stretching back in a series of thatched platforms. Indonesian, seafood, pizza, pasta and vegetarian dishes. Special dishes each night and on Sunday there is an evening buffet of regional dishes. Try the 'death by chocolate' dessert. Reservations necessary.

✉ Monkey Forest Rd ☎ 0361-975447 🕐 10–10

Cahaya Dewata Restaurant (£££)
Transport needed to get here from central Ubud. Reserve a window table overlooking the gorge; there are great views at lunchtime, river sounds and twinkling lights of Denpasar at night. Indonesian, Japanese and European dishes. Salads and guacamole for appetizers.

✉ Cahaya Dewata Hotel, Kedewatan ☎ 0361-975495 🕐 7:30–10

Casa Luna (£)
Wholesome Balinese food and some steaks, salads, excellent bread and vegetarian choices. Recommended for breakfast, lunch or dinner. Try for a table at the back for a river view. Balinese cooking courses are organised by the restaurant.

✉ Jalan Raya ☎ 0361-96283 🕐 8–10

The Globetrotter (££)
A little out of the way but there is free pick-up-and-return transportation. International food in a bistro setting.

✉ Jalan Raya Andong, Petulu ☎ 0361-96129 🕐 11–11. Closed: Monday

Hotel Tjampuhan Restaurant (££)
Arrive before dark and take a stroll around the beautiful grounds before retiring to the restaurant. Regional and international food served in this famous old hotel.

✉ Jalan Raya Campuhan, Hotel Tjampuhan ☎ 0361-975368 🕐 8–10

Ibu Rai (£)
Centrally located for people-watching on the street. Balinese dishes, spaghetti, seafood, wine.

✉ 72 Monkey Forest Rd ☎ 0361-975066 🕐 9–10

The Best Restaurant?
The Café Wayan restaurant was started in 1977 when Wayan Kelepon opened her own *warung* (inexpensive roadside restaurant or street stall). She sold rice to fellow Ubud residents, and soft drinks to passing tourists. Ten years later she opened Café Wayan with four tables. Now there are forty-five tables and that's not enough to satisfy the demand. It is probably the best restaurant in Ubud and one of the best in all of Bali.

Ubud is Best

Ubud offers better value in quality dining than anywhere else in Bali or Lombok. Not even the sumptuous restaurants that adorn the top-class hotels of Nusa Dua can provide an equally accomplished range of international and local dishes and serve them in an appropriate atmosphere of artistic aplomb.

Kokokan Club (££)

Delicious Thai food served in this well-established hotel restaurant that manages to create a refined atmosphere without pretensions or high prices.

✉ **Jalan Pengosekan, Puri Indah Hotel** ☎ **0361-975742** 🕙 **11–10**

Luchu Bar & Restaurant (£)

Unassuming café with a happy hour (5–7) and a wide choice of regional dishes, steaks and seafood.

✉ **Monkey Forest Road** ☎ **0361-974226** 🕙 **9–11**

Mumbul's (£)

Indian and Balinese dishes, very suitable for vegetarians, next door to Ubud Palace. Come here for something novel like spicy roasted *tempeh* (fermented bean curd) in pitta bread, or just a *thali* (a complete Indian meal served on a metal plate and sectioned into different dishes).

✉ **Jalan Raya** ☎ **0361-975364** 🕙 **11–10**

Murni's Warung (££)

Two levels with tables overlooking a river and tropical greenery. Mediterranean and Indonesian food, and curries. Give a day's notice for a Balinese feast of smoked duck.

✉ **Jalan Raya, Campuhan** ☎ **0361-975282** 🕙 **8:30–10**

Nomad Bar & Restaurant (£)

Appetizers and main courses of fish, chicken, steaks and local dishes, such as *pepesikan* (grilled fish with herbs in a banana leaf with salad and rice).

✉ **Jalan Raya (opposite the playing field)** ☎ **0361-975721** 🕙 **9–11**

Parkit Restaurant (££)

A hotel restaurant serving Balinese and international food. Free transportation available in Central Ubud.

✉ **Heritage Champlung Sari Hotel, Monkey Forest Road** ☎ **0361-975418** 🕙 **8–10**

Pita Maha Terrace Restaurant (££–£££)

Alfresco dining in a beautiful setting overlooking the valley of the Wos river. International and traditional specialities; a day's notice needed for roasted duck.

✉ **Jalan Sanggingan, Pita Maha Hotel** ☎ **0361-974330** 🕙 **10–10**

Puri's Bar & Restaurant (£)

An unpretentious place on the main road. There is noise from traffic sometimes, but this place is a handy antidote to shopping fatique and close to Puri Saren Agung (► 55) for evening dances. Light meals as well as meat and vegetable dishes. Good value drinks.

✉ **Jalan Raya** 🕙 **8–10**

Purimuwa (£)

Menus in English and German explain the Balinese dishes in detail. Try for a table at the back in the garden.

✉ **Monkey Forest Rd** ☎ **0361-975441** 🕙 **8–10**

Ryoshi (££)

Japanese restaurant, serving sushi and tempura dishes.

✉ **Jalan Raya** ☎ **0361-976362** 🕙 **12–12**

Saffron (££)

A new restaurant, specialising in oriental curries.

✉ **Banyan Tree Hotel, Jalan Tegallalang, Banjar Nagi** ☎ **0361-975825** 🕙 **6:30–10:30**

North & East Bali

When it comes to the Lake Batur area there tends to be an inverse relationship between the quality of the food and the popularity of the destination. The sheer number of coach tours that disgorge hungry sightseers every lunchtime has led to a surfeit of plush and overpriced restaurants offering pre-cooked buffet lunches. With your own transport it is possible to escape by driving north from Penelokan towards Kintamani and looking for somewhere like Puncak Sari (➤ 58) where the food will not be wonderfully different but where there is more space and less people. Another possibility is the road in Toya Bungkah where there are a number of inexpensive and reasonably priced restaurants offering better food than anywhere in Penelokan itself.

In the north of Bali the best place to eat is undoubtedly Lovina. There are countless places to choose from on either side of the road and, tucked away down the side streets leading to the beach, there are plenty of inexpensive restaurants belonging to the homestays. There is healthy competition between the various establishments in Lovina and you can wander from one place to another checking menus and comparing prices. The actual differences in the cost of a meal need only concern those on a very tight budget; the availability of particular types of fresh fish is a more important consideration.

Singaraja may be the second largest city in Bali but from the visitor's point of view this is not reflected in the restaurant scene. The only place where a cluster of restaurants may be found is around a small square off Jalan Jen Achmad Yani near the corner with Jalan Pramuka. One of the best restaurants here is Gandi (➤ 98) but there are other places in this centrally located square worth considering.

Lovina

Aryas Cafe (£)
The Aryas café is a modest establishment with local dishes and some vegetarian choices, good desserts.
✉ **Kalibukbuk** ☎ **0362-41797**
🕐 **8:30–11**

Astina (£)
Just 500m off the main road, within spitting distance of the beach, this restaurant serves inexpensive and simple food in modest surroundings.
✉ **Kalibukbuk** ☎ **0362-41187**
🕐 **7:30–10**

Las Palmas (£–££)
Pleasant beach-side hotel restaurant with Indian, Chinese and European food. Set in its own grounds with lush gardens.
✉ **Palma Beach Hotel**
☎ **0362-41775** 🕐 **7–10**

Lian Seafood Restaurant (££)
Opposite the Aditya bungalows and not on the beach side of road, but the seafood (squid, crab, lobster and prawn) is very good. Local wine available. Husband in the kitchen, wife serving.
✉ **Kaliasem, just west of Kalibukbuk** ☎ **0362-41480**
🕐 **10–11**

A *Warung*
A *warung* has no exact translation – food stall, transport café, take-away – just think of it as a poor person's restaurant. It may be a rough shed with a few tables or perhaps on wheels at the side of the pavement. A night market is often the best place to be adventurous and try some of the pure Indonesian food they offer; just point to something that looks interesting – *cap cai* (cooked vegetables) or *nasi goreng* (fried rice).

Lovina

The restaurant scene in the north of Bali is to be found in the beach-resort area of Lovina, a few miles west of Singaraja. Lovina stretches indeterminately for over 9km but most places to eat are clustered either side of the village of Kalibukbuk, which is situated on the main road. Here you will find more than a dozen restaurants, many of them specialising in fish dishes and all of them offering good value for money.

Malibu (£)

One of the liveliest restaurants in Lovina with live music from 10PM to 1AM. Telephone to ask about free transport. The food is not wonderful but there is a great choice and the drinks list is very satisfying. Good for breakfast also.

✉ **Kalibukbuk** ☎ **0362-41671** 🕐 **8–1**

Mandhara Chico (£)

This hotel and restaurant is at the eastern end of Lovina, opposite the petrol station. The restaurant is a cut above the usual budget places dotted between here and Kalibukbuk. Tourist fare.

✉ **Anturan, 5km east of Kalibukbuk** ☎ **0362-41476** 🕐 **7:30–10**

Puri-Bali (£)

The restaurant belonging to Puri-Bali Bungalows is very close to the beach and mostly serves seafood and steaks. Relaxing and informal.

✉ **Kalibukbuk** ☎ **0362-41485** 🕐 **7:30–10**

Tanjung Alam (£)

You can't get any closer to the beach than this – waves almost lap over the tables! Come here for an evening meal and watch the sun go down. Seafood and European dishes.

✉ **Kaliasem, just west of Kalibukbuk** ☎ **0362-41223** 🕐 **10–10**

Penelokan

Puncak Sari (£)

Penelokan is not short of restaurants offering lunch buffets but one large coach party can take them over. This restaurant is outside the centre so there is less risk of congestion and the view from the outside tables is spectacular.

✉ **2km north of Penelokan on road to Kintamani** ☎ **0366-51073** 🕐 **10–4**

Singaraja

Gandi (£)

An unpretentious restaurant located just off the main street away from the traffic noise. Mostly Indonesian and Chinese dishes with vegetarian choices. Its popularity with the locals is the best recommendation.

✉ **25 Jalan Jen Achmad Yani** ☎ **0362-21163** 🕐 **8–8**

Tirtagangga

Tirta Ayu (£)

It is worth timing your visit to the Water Palace in Tirtagangga (➤ 24) so that you can enjoy a meal at the Tirta Ayu restaurant inside its grounds. The food is not especially good, but the delightful setting overlooking the pools and greenery makes this the best place for a meal in this corner of Bali.

✉ **Water Palace** ☎ **0363-21697** 🕐 **7–6**

Toya Bungkah (Lake Batur)

Under the Volcano (£)

There are two restaurants and hotels with this name, just a few hundred metres apart, situated close to the shore of Lake Batur. Under the same management, the restaurants offer better food than most of the local competition. Regional and Western dishes.

✉ **Toya Bungkah** 🕐 **7–10**

Lombok

Gili Trawangan

Restoran Borobudur (£)
Centrally located next to the main cluster of shops. Very popular, seafood, steak, Indonesian dishes.
✉ **Close to point where boats dock** 🕐 7:30–10

Sunset (£)
Located further south than the main concentration of restaurants, this restaurant is handy after climbing the nearby hill. Simple pasta and chicken dishes, sandwiches and omelettes.
✉ **South end of island, facing the sea** 🕐 8–11

Kuta

Kuta Indah Hotel Restaurant (££)
This is a spanking new hotel and restaurant within walking distance of a lovely beach. No surprises in the menu but, until the big new resorts take over, this is the best place for a meal in southern Lombok.
✉ **Kuta Indah Hotel, Kuta** ☎ 0370-54628 🕐 7–10

Senggigi

Blue Coral (££)
Friendly, candlelit tables but informal, attached to diving school of same name on the main street. Meat, seafood and Japanese food (but skip the pizza).
✉ **Jalan Raya Senggigi** ☎ 0370-93033 🕐 8–11

Kafé Alberto (££)
Located in the Art Market, serving pizzas, Indonesian food and barbecues. Touristy but superb sea views.
✉ **Jalan Raya Senggigi** ☎ 0370-93758 🕐 10–10

Kartika Senggigi (£)
Vast menu with some interesting specialities like sautéed tofu with local fish. Squid, lobster, prawn, crab and satay.
✉ **Jalan Raya Senggigi** ☎ 0370-93228 🕐 9–10:30

Kebun Rohani (££)
Pleasing little restaurant, close to the Sheraton, specialising in barbecued seafood.
✉ **Jalan Raya Senggigi** ☎ 0370-93018 🕐 7:30–10

Naga (££)
Belonging to a split-site hotel, the Naga restaurant is situated on the inland side of the road opposite the beach-facing accommodation. Chinese, seafood and Thai food.
✉ **Jalan Raya Senggigi** ☎ 0370-93101 🕐 10–10

Princess of Lombok (££)
Mexican favourites and steaks, poor choice of desserts. A pub downstairs with darts and billiards.
✉ **Jalan Raya Senggigi** ☎ 0370-93011 🕐 7:30–11

Sunshine Restaurant (£)
An informal Chinese seafood restaurant facing the sea. The day trips to Gili Trawangan depart near by. Good value.
✉ **Jalan Raya Senggigi** ☎ 0370-932232 🕐 8–10

Tetebatu

Soedjono Hotel Restaurant (£)
The restaurant has picturesque views over the thatched roofs of the hotel's bungalows to the rice paddies beyond. Indonesian food.
✉ **Soedjono Hotel, Tetebatu** (► 103) ☎ 0370-22159 🕐 6:30–11

The Rambutan
The rambutan is sometimes known as the hairy lychee ('rambat' is Indonesian for hair) because the actual fruit is very similar in its taste. Don't be alarmed when confronted with the startlingly red (and very hairy) skin, simply peel it off and eat the pearl white fruit within. Avoid the seed in its centre, it is said to be narcotic!

South & Southeast Bali

Prices
Prices are approximate, based on a room per night, regardless of single or double occupancy:

£   = under Rp55,500
££ = Rp55,500–129,500
£££ = over Rp129,500

Candi Dasa

Amankila (£££)
The Amankila hotel boasts thirty-five rooms starting at Rp925,000 (or about US$400) a night, exclusively located on a beachfront plateau with spectacular views of the Indian Ocean. The tiered swimming pool is unique on Bali, the suites are luxurious.
✉ **Manggis, (PO Box 133, Klungkung 80701)** ☎ **0363-41333**

Candi Dasa Ashram (££)
This is an ashram (a place of religious retreat) and guests may participate in some of the meditation sessions, but there is no obligation. All meals are strictly vegetarian and are included in the room rate. The ashram has a splendid location close to the beach. No hot water.
✉ **Off Candi Dasa's main road, next to a lagoon** ☎ **0363-41108**

Ida Candi Dasa (£)
Bungalows with verandas, fans and cold water, looking out onto a pretty garden that reaches down to the sea. Breakfast served in the rooms. Ida Candi Dasa is one of the best budget places in Candi Dasa.
✉ **Entrance on Candi Dasa's main road** ☎ **No phone**

Kelapa Mas (£)
Kelapa Mas is located right on the beach with a traditional Balinese garden, friendly staff and a restaurant. There is hot water, but no air-conditioning. Suitable for families.
✉ **Candi Dasa Beach, (PO Box 103, Amlapura 80801)** ☎ **0363-41947**

Kuta-Legian

Agung Cottages (££)
In the very heart of Kuta. Most rooms have air-conditioning but less expensive rooms without air-conditioning (but with fans) are also available. You can't get more central than this.
✉ **Jalan Legian** ☎ **0361-757427**

Bali Garden (£££)
Popular with Australians, within walking distance of Kuta's beach, shops, bars and restaurants.
✉ **Jalan Kartika, (PO Box 1101)** ☎ **0361-752725**

Bali Indah (£)
Basic but very inexpensive. A bed, shower and toilet.
✉ **Poppies Lane 11** ☎ **0361-752509**

Bali Padma (£££)
Top-notch hotel in Legian, over 400 rooms, with one of the best tropical gardens of any hotel in Bali.
✉ **Corner of Jalan Pantai Kuta and Jalan Melasti** ☎ **0361-751891**

Karthi Inn (££)
Three levels with all the rooms overlooking the swimming pool. Well located for shopping expeditions in Kuta.
✉ **Jalan Kartika Plaza** ☎ **0361-754810**

Marsa Inn (£–££)
A haven of peace in the middle of Kuta, with a choice of rooms with or without air-conditioning.
✉ **Poppies Lane 1** ☎ **0361-758507**

Natour Kuta Beach (£££)

The only hotel with direct access to the beach, an advantage of being built on the site of the first hotel in Kuta. The original hotel was begun by an American couple and prospered until World War II (► 38).

✉ Jalan Pantai No 1, (PO Box 3393) ☎ 0361-751361

Okie House (£)

Tucked away down a lane off Jalan Legian, the Okie House is good budget accommodation. Clean rooms, hot water and a fan; breakfast included.

✉ Poppies Lane 11, Jalan Legian ☎ 0361-752081

Poppies Cottages 1 (££–£££)

Despite being in the centre of Kuta, this delightful hotel manages to maintain an air of calm. Thatched cottages set in lovely secluded gardens and there is a good swimming pool.

✉ Poppies Lane 1 ☎ 0361-751059

Nusa Dua

Amanusa (£££)

Set apart – and not just physically – from the other Nusa Dua resort hotels. Like the other two Aman resorts in Bali, the architecture, decor and views are outstanding and unsurpassed.

✉ Nusa Dua ☎ 0361-72333

Bali Hilton (£££)

At the southern end of the beach, with the full range of amenities and facilities. Good restaurants and reliable service.

✉ PO Box 46, Nusa Dua ☎ 0361-771102

Melici Bali (£££)

This Spanish-run hotel group has over 500 rooms here, set amongst 10 hectares of lush gardens. Recently renovated, good restaurants and sports facilities.

✉ Kawasan Wisata BTDC Lot 1, Nusa Dua ☎ 0361-771510

Sheraton Laguna (£££)

The ultimate swimming pool, complete with sandy beaches and waterfalls, with a hotel built around it. The best rooms have direct access to the pool. A real playground of a hotel.

✉ PO Box 17, Nusa Dua Beach ☎ 0361-771327

Sanur

Bali Hyatt (£££)

Occupying 14 hectares between the beach and the road. The tropical opulence of the gardens and architecture is impressive and there are five restaurants to choose from.

✉ Jalan Danau Tamblingan ☎ 0361-288361

Hotel Sanur Aerowisata (£££)

At the southern end of the beach, this huge hotel has all the luxuries necessary for a lazy beach holiday.

✉ Jalan Danau Tamblingan ☎ 0361-288011

Tirtagangga

Tirta Ayu Homestay (£)

Situated inside the Water Palace, with one very good room with a fan and delightful private outdoor shower. Other rooms with plain indoor showers. The climate is cooler here.

✉ Tirtagangga ☎ 0363-21697

The Best?

What is the best hotel in Bali? If your priority is a swimming pool then the Sheraton Lagoona (a pool with a hotel around the edges ► 101) and Amankila (exquisite tiered pools and an olympic-sized one ► 100) are close competitors. For Balinese ambience and luxury the Pita Maha in Ubud (► 102) is hard to beat. For a sense of history try the nearby Hotel Tjampuhan (► 102). For sheer class and sublimely good taste it is hard to beat any one of the three Aman hotels: Amankila (► 100), Amanusa (► 101), Amandari (► 102).

Central & West Bali

Hotels and _Losmen_
Accommodation places that call themselves hotels are usually the larger establishments where one can expect a swimming pool and air-conditioning in all the rooms. Smaller places are often called _losmen_ or homestays because the proprietor usually lives close by and there is often a choice of rooms and cottages with or without air-conditioning.

Ubud and Surrounding Area

Amandari (£££)
Another of the three Aman luxury hotels in Bali. The suites are elegantly beautiful, the atmosphere one of sublime indulgence, and the views are fabulous.
✉ **Sayan/Kedewatan**
☎ **0362-975333**

Bali Spirit (£££)
In a peaceful rural area outside of Ubud in the valley of the Wos River with superb views. The traditional art and furnishings include imaginative touches to the rooms, like the bathrooms artistically designed with inlaid stone. Spa services, massages, swimming pool, beauty salon, and free transport around the Ubud area for shopping, dining and dance performances.
✉ **Nyuhkuning, PO Box 189, Ubud 80571** ☎ **0361-974012**

Cahaya Dewata (£££)
The deluxe rooms all overlook River Ayung at Kedewatan village. The standard rooms have garden views. Smallish pool. It helps to have your own transport as it is too far to walk between the hotel and central Ubud and there are plenty of art galleries along the road.
✉ **Kedewatan** ☎ **0361-975495**

Gerebig Bungalows (£)
Excellent accommodation in the delightful village of Penestanan. Clean rooms with balconies overlooking rice fields, 30m off the main road through the village.
✉ **Penestanan, PO Box 212, Ubud** ☎ **0361-974582**

Hotel Tjampuhan (£££)
Cottage accommodation with verandas overlooking a picturesque valley, built around the home of artist Walter Spies, whose 1930s house is one of the more expensive rooms. The gardens are exquisite.
✉ **Jalan Raya Campuhan, PO Box 198, Ubud 80571** ☎ **0361-975368**

Pertiwi Bungalows (££)
Centrally located, halfway down Monkey Forest Road, with relaxing gardens, rooms with balconies and Balinese decor, and a medium-sized pool.
✉ **Monkey Forest Road** ☎ **0361-975236**

Pita Maha (£££)
A new luxury hotel with beautifully designed villas and tasteful Balinese decor. One of the most luxurious and elegant hotels in Bali. Free bus to and from town.
✉ **Jalan Sanggingan, PO Box 198, Ubud 80571** ☎ **0361-974330**

Puri Bunga Village Hotel (£££)
Picturesque location overlooking River Ayung. Small swimming pool but terrific views from the rooms. Transport needed to reach central Ubud.
✉ **Kedewatan** ☎ **0361-975488**

Wartini (£)
A good example of a typical Ubud homestay with a friendly atmosphere and good rooms. Tucked away down a side street off the main road through Peliatan.
✉ **Off Jalan Raya, Peliatan** ☎ **0361-96281**

North & East Bali & Lombok

North and East Bali

Lovina
Aditya Bungalows (££)
Air-conditioned cottages with verandas and good facilities – all for a lot less than you'd pay in southern Bali. Swimming pool.
✉ **Kaliasem** ☎ **0362-41059**

Bali Lovina Beach Cottages (££)
Balinese-style cottages stretching down to the sea, with air-conditioning, swimming pool and pool-side bar.
✉ **Pantai Lovina** ☎ **0362-41285**

Palma Beach Hotel (££)
Close to a shallow stretch of beach that is safe for swimming and children. Lots of facilities, swimming pool.
✉ **Jalan Raya** ☎ **0362-41775**

Rambutan Beach Cottages (£–££)
Attractive beach-side cottages set in a tropical garden complete with swimming pool. Choice of rooms with or without hot water, no air-conditioning. Good restaurant.
✉ **Kalibukbuk** ☎ **0362-41388**

Taman Lily's (£)
Six new, elegant cottages with verandas facing a small garden. Hot water, but no air–conditioning. By the beach.
✉ **Kalibukbuk** ☎ **0362-41307**

Lombok

Kuta
Kuta Indah (£–££)
Close to the beach and surrounding hills, this is the first of many new hotels that will eventually colonise this corner of Lombok. Functional rooms.
✉ **Kuta** ☎ **0370-54628**

Senggigi
Kebun Rohani (£)
Thatched bamboo cottages. Mosquito nets and a mattress, breakfast included.
✉ **Jalan Senggigi** ☎ **0370-93018**

Graha Senggigi Beach Hotel (££)
One of the best Senggigi resort hotels.
✉ **Jalan Raya Senggigi** ☎ **0370-93101**

Lombok Intan Laguna (£££)
Good facilities, including tennis, gym and sauna, swimming pool and a restaurant open 24 hours.
✉ **Jalan Raya Senggigi** ☎ **0370-93090**

Pondok Shinta (£)
Very basic (bed, shower and small fan) and very inexpensive rooms. Easy access to the beach.
✉ **Jalan Raya Senggigi** ☎ **0370-93012**

Sheraton Senggigi (£££)
Perfect beach location with good shade and a pool that children will love.
✉ **Jalan Raya Senggigi.** ☎ **0370-93333**

Suranadi
Suranadi Hotel
Once a Dutch residence, this hotel has pleasant grounds, a tennis court and a spring-water swimming pool.
✉ **7km north of Narmada** ☎ **0370-33686**

Tetebatu
Soedjono Hotel (£)
Built in the 1930s as a private home, frequented by the Dutch, and a hotel since 1983. Spring-water swimming pool.
✉ **Tetebatu, Sikur** ☎ **0370-22159**

Accommodation in Lombok
Visitors staying in less expensive accommodation in Lombok will miss the decor and craftwork of Ubud homestays and their small touches like the complimentary flask of tea. A lot of accommodation in Senggigi is in modern hotels with comfortable rooms and facilities like swimming pools and the rest of the island is developing along similar lines. The best place for budget rooms is the Gili Islands.

Balinese Paintings

Paintings

The range and quality of paintings for sale in Ubud is astonishing and it pays to shop around before making a decision. If the painting is purchased in its frame there may be a problem accommodating it into your luggage, so consider negotiating a price without a frame and have the painting wrapped inside a sturdy cardboard roll. Nearly all the galleries will be happy to do this.

Ubud and Surrounding Area

Agung Rai

The Agung Rai gallery is probably the most famous and reputable place in Ubud. There are seven galleries in all here with high-quality paintings ranging in price from Rp50,000 to Rp115,625,000 (or about US$50,000).

✉ **Jalan Peliatan** ☎ **0361-975449**

Ibu Rai

Ibu Rai is an artist specialising in modern themes. Some negotiation over prices is possible.

✉ **Monkey Forest Road**
☎ **0361-975066**

I Nyoman Jerit

One of the first galleries on the left upon entering Penestanan from Campuan, two shops away from the Sri Ratih cottages. The prices are not outrageous.

✉ **Penestanan, Ubud**
☎ **No phone**

K Sudana

K Sudana is an artist who tends to like painting faces but there is other material on display.

✉ **Jalan Raya Campuhan, just beyond the Pita Maha hotel**
☎ **0361-975731**

Komaneka

One of the more upmarket galleries in Ubud with an excellent range of quality paintings. Make sure you take a look at the visitors' book as it makes interesting reading. Prices begin around Rp230,000 (or about

US$100) and 20 per cent discount is the most you can hope for.

✉ **Monkey Forest Road**
☎ **0361-976090**

Rahmat Agung

A group of three painters display their work for sale at the Rahmat Agung and it is worth a browse, although the quality ranges quite a lot. Bargain for around 40 per cent off the first price that is quoted.

✉ **Jalan Sanggingan**
☎ **No phone**

Sunari

The Sunari gallery is close to the Neka Museum, on the other side of the road, and has a fair selection of different styles of paintings for sale.

✉ **Jalan Raya Sanggingan**
☎ **0361-975808**

Wayan Wijaya

If walking in Campuan (▶ 54) this small painter's studio is worth a visit. In addition to the usual scenes of village life, there are also some interesting modern themes. Expect to pay from Rp92,500 (or about US$40) for a canvas.

✉ **Payogan, Ubud**
☎ **No phone**

Varia

There may be not be any masterpieces here but there is a reasonable selection, including some whimsical frogs cavorting in a Balinese landscape and immense canvases of tropical plants . Expect a 40 per cent discount.

✉ **Jalan Sanggingan**
☎ **No phone**

Jewellery

Celuk

Dharma Putra Silver
In the middle of the village. A big selection but it helps to have some idea of prices before entering into negotiations here.
✉ Celuk ☎ 0361-298634

Indarti Silver
On the left-hand side shortly after entering the village from Ubud, the stock is mostly earrings.
✉ Celuk ☎ 0361-298172

Murti I
In the middle of the village, this shop has interesting designs. Expect a 50 per cent discount.
✉ Celuk ☎ 0361-298018

Kuta

Jonathan Gallery
A reputable shop selling gold and silver jewellery. Fixed prices in US dollars.
✉ 109 Jalan Legian ☎ 0361-754209

Suarti
The imaginative window displays single out these jewellery shops. As well as the two outlets listed below, there are Suarti shops at the Mastapa Garden Hotel, Jalan Legian, Kuta (☎ 0361-751660), and at 404 Jalan Legian, Legian (☎ 0361-756094) and also on Monkey Forest Road, Ubud (☎ 0361-974194).
✉ Jalan Bakung Sari and Poppies Lane 11 ☎ 0361-754899

Yusuf's Silver
Another reputable shop along Jalan Legian. All the prices of rings, earrings and chains are fixed.
✉ 85 Jalan Legian ☎ 0361-752050

Ubud

Ayu Silver
Reasonably priced bangles, bracelets and rings. Bargaining required.
✉ Monkey Forest Road ☎ 0361-96370

Putra Silver
Three outlets in Ubud, all with fixed prices (which saves a lot of time). Rings, earrings, bracelets and chains.
✉ Monkey Forest Rd, Ubud ☎ 0361-975178

Ubud Corner
The same merchandise tends to turn up again and again in many of the jewellery shops, but this shop has more original necklaces and earrings. Prices are fixed but ask for 10 per cent discount if purchasing two items.
✉ Monkey Forest Road ☎ 0361-974009

Lombok

Senggigi
Apart from a small selection in Senggigi's Art Market and Pacific Supermarket (▶ 107), there is little in the way of jewellery for sale in Lombok. However, at the southern end of Senggigi's main street there are two or three very small shops, with no names to their stores, selling bangles and necklaces made from bone and coloured stones. The more interesting items come from other Indonesian islands to the east of Lombok.
✉ Jalan Raya Senggigi

Choose with Care
Celuk and Kuta are the two best places for buying jewellery and many people think that some of Kuta's shops are able to offer the more imaginative and original designs. In both places, though, look for sturdily made pieces and avoid those that look as if they could easily come apart (because they probably will!). The sturdiness of the product is as important a consideration as the price when purchasing jewellery in Bali.

Arts & Crafts

Negotiating Skills
Shopping in Bali or Lombok requires bargaining skills and many inexperienced visitors end up regretting the prices they paid for their early purchases. If time allows, delay a purchase until different prices have been compared for similar goods, and as a general rule try to avoid making your offer (which you can never reduce) until the seller makes at least one reduction on their opening price.

Banjar Tega

Bali Spice
When visiting the hot springs west of Lovina at Banjar Tega (► 70) stock up on supplies of spices not so readily available back home – saffron, vanilla, tamarind and black chillies.

✉ **Outside the entrance to the hot springs** ☎ **No phone**

Candi Dasa

Asri
Masks, batik cloth, woodcarvings, mirrors, decorated frames and so on. Reasonable prices, all fixed. Open until 11PM.

✉ **Jalan Raya Candi Dasa**
☎ **0363-41098**

Kuta

Golden Buffalo
It claims to have the biggest range of bronze products in all of Indonesia, so you should find what you are looking for. There is also a branch along Monkey Forest Road in Ubud.

✉ **1A Jalan Padma Timur**
☎ **0361-755936**

Sedana Pertiwi
Chess sets, wind chimes, wooden flowers, decorations for the home and souvenirs.

✉ **Jalan Buni Sari** ☎ **0361-751758**

Shopping Complex
Entered opposite the Bali Garden Hotel and close to McDonald's, this pedestrian-ised precinct has a number of upmarket jewellery and antique shops, boutiques and art-and-crafts places. They all have fixed prices.

✉ **Jalan Kartika Plaza**

Uma
The shop is virtually dedicated to candle stands. Also some letter holders, frames and mirrors.

✉ **355 Jalan Legian** ☎ **0361-757743**

Mas

Adhi
One of the big arts-and-crafts shops in Mas. Hundreds of resplendent masks and wooden fruits, from single apples to an entire pineapple tree! Prices are marked but negotiable.

✉ **Main road through Mas, at the Ubud end** ☎ **0361-975228**

Pantheon Gallery
Approaching Mas from the south, this is one of the first mansion-like shops on the left-hand side of the road. Expect 50 per cent off the first price given for the Buddhas, statues and wall hangings but aim as high as a 70 per cent discount.

✉ **Main road through Mas, southern end** ☎ **0361-975224**

Villa Interiors
Quality furniture, including bureaux and chairs, and smaller items for the home, such as stationery boxes. Shipping is arranged for larger items.

✉ **Jalan Raya** ☎ **0361-974050**

Penujak, Lombok

Mandalika
One of the specialist shops in the pottery village of Penujak in Lombok. Mostly pots in a variety of sizes but also some lamps, ashtrays and nice plates with fish designs.

✉ **Jalan Selong Blanak**
☎ **No phone**

Sanur

Art Market
Stalls selling a wide choice of arts and crafts: masks, woodcarvings, screen-printed fans, batik shirts and so on.

✉ **Northern end of Jalan Danau Tamblingan**

Asano Art & Craft
Expensive but exquisite sewing boxes are typical of the quality products here.

✉ **69 Jalan Danau Tamblingan**
☎ **0361-289441**

Senggigi, Lombok

Art Market
A shopping complex, close to the Sheraton hotel. Bargaining is necessary.

✉ **Jalan Raya Senggigi**

Asmara Art Shop
One of the better art shops in Lombok, at the Sheraton end of the village. Baskets, cloth, pottery and wood carvings.

✉ **Jalan Raya Senggigi**
☎ **0370-93109**

Pacific Supermarket
The upper level of this huge supermarket, at the Sheraton hotel end of the main road, is devoted to arts and crafts from all over Lombok. The quality is generally poor but this is a good place to visit to get some idea of prices before bargaining elsewhere.

✉ **Jalan Raya Senggigi**
☎ **0370-93120**

Tampaksiring

Mawar
Situated at the Ubud end of this long village, all the products are made from wood – decorative cats and dogs, fruit, coconut earrings and lots more. Inexpensive.

✉ **Tampaksiring** ☎ **0361-901256**

Ubud and Surrounding Area

The Duck Man of Bali
A famous store on the main road between Ubud and Gianyar, close to Goa Gajah. The shop sells wooden ducks – hundreds of them in all sizes and colours. The prices reflect the sizes and range from Rp20,000 to Rp5,000,000. The cheaper quackers are upstairs.

✉ **Tengkulak Kaja, Jalan Goa Gajah** ☎ **0361-975305**

Made Budiasa
Wood carvings ranging in size from small dancing frogs to massive demons that require a freight service to ship home. Easily found on the main road from Ubud to Gianyar, just past the turn-off to Denpasar.

✉ **Jalan Goa Gajah** ☎ **0361-976082**

Rai Sandi
Close to the Pita Maha hotel, this shop specialises in colourful masks and ceiling-hanging figures of Balinese dancers.

✉ **Jalan Raya Campuhan**
☎ **0361-975119**

Wora Shop
Halfway down the road on the left-hand side from the Puri Saren Agung end, this shop specialises in *ikat* wall hangings and various 'antiques'. Prices can be expensive.

✉ **Monkey Forest Road**
☎ **0361-975675**

Shipments Home
Serious shoppers face the problem of transporting home a purchase too big or heavy for the airplane. In Kuta there are agents specialising in shipping home purchases, but the better shops will be able to make the arrangements for you. Expect to pay around Rp580,000 (or about US$250) per cubic metre for shipments to Europe, more for the United States. Other considerations include insurance, import duties, and the fact that wood products may crack when exported to drier climates. Ceramics fired at low temperatures are particularly fragile.

Clothes

Ikat Cloth
Ikat is a traditional southeast Asian method of patterning cloth so that complex patterns of colours can be built up through the weaving process. Its most distinguishable characteristic is the fuzzy blurring of one colour into another, caused by the different dyes bleeding into one another.

Kuta

Art Market
There are numerous stalls and small shops with their wares flowing out onto the pavement, but there is no art to be found in this market. Instead you can browse through the colourfully patterned beach dresses and shorts, racks of baggy cotton pants and T-shirts.
📧 **End of Jalan Bakung Sari, near the beach**

Pusaka
This shop sells quality T-shirts with interesting designs. It also stocks batik cloth. Batik cloth has colourful designs produced by applying wax to the parts to be left untreated. Pusaka is located at the top end of Jalan Legian, not far from the vegetarian Aromas Café (► 92).
📧 **338 Jalan Legian**
📞 **No phone**

Studio
One of the best clothes shops in Bali, especially for women as the men's section is mostly smart T-shirts and beach shorts. Studio also have an outlet in the Galleria in Nusa Dua (see below).
📧 **Kuta Square, Jalan Pantai Kuta** 📞 **0361-752717**

Uluwatu
Dresses and blouses (and sheets and pillow cases) made from hand-made Balinese lace. Good quality hand-made lace-work should withstand repeated washings. Apart from the Kuta shop listed here there is also a branch in Galleria Nusa Dua (► 109).

📧 **Jalan Legian, near Poppies Lane** 📞 **0361 751933**

Nusa Dua

Studio
This is one of the best clothes stores in the Galleria shopping complex (► 109) and a sister shop to Studio in Kuta (see above), with a similar selection of quality women's clothes.
📧 **Galleria Nusa Dua, Block A5** 📞 **0361-773502**

Sukarara, Lombok

Dharma Setya
Ikat cloth, priced according to quality (which varies from the mediocre to the outstanding). The workshop is in a separate building and can be visited.
📧 **Jalan Tenun** 📞 **0370-54870**

Ubud and Surrounding Area

Bagus
Bagus is one of the few clothes shops outside of the Kuta area with a stock that goes beyond T-shirts, shorts, and cheap dresses that lose their colour after a few washes. It has mostly rayon and cotton dresses, blouses and some matching sets. Sizes can be made to order in two days.
📧 **Jalan Dewi Sita** 📞 **0361-976611**

Wardani's Shop
Wardini's shop sells clothing, hand-woven material and silk, all at reasonable prices.
📧 **Monkey Forest Road**
📞 **0361-975538**

Miscellaneous

Candi Dasa

Candi Bookstore
The best selection of second-hand books outside of Kuta. English, German, French, Swedish, Dutch and Italian editions, plus a few others.
✉ **45 Jalan Raya Candi Dasa**
☎ **No phone**

Kuta

Billabong
One of the many specialist surfers' shops in Kuta selling surfing gear and garments.
✉ **16 Jalan Buni Sari**
☎ **0361-752219**

Matahari Department Stores
There are two department stores, both selling clothes, jewellery, watches and everything else you would expect to find in a super-market. Fixed prices and air-conditioning are the advantages to browsing through the four floors of the Kuta Square branch. The Legian Plaza has three floors. Open until 10:30PM.
✉ **Legian Plaza, Jalan Legian and Kuta Square**

Nusa Dua

Galleria
A little soulless but a very convenient shopping complex in Nusa Dua. Jewellers, a supermarket, sports wear, an optician and designer-wear boutiques. Free shuttle buses to and from all the Nusa Dua hotels.
✉ **Nusa Dua** ☎ **0361-771662**

Galeri Keris
This department store has a full range of wood carvings, and other art and crafts, as well as fabrics, perfume and clothes. Useful for establishing prices or for buying last-minute souvenirs and presents.
✉ **Galleria** ☎ **0361-771303**

Sheraton Nusa Indah Shopping Arcade
The Sheraton Nusa Indah has a better selection of shops than the other hotels in Nusa Dua. Clothes, fashion accessories, crafts and jewellery make up the content of most of the upmarket shops.
✉ **Sheraton Nusa Indah Hotel**

Sanur

Bali Harum
A gift shop with above-average merchandise. There are also outlets in Jalan Legian Tengah in Legian and in Jalan Raya in Seminyak.
✉ **Jalan Danau Tamblingan**
☎ **0361-286475**

Ubud and Surrounding Area

Adinda
The word *adinda* means 'cute little sister/brother' and this is a cute shop for young girls and boys. *Takraw* balls (*Takraw* is a southeast Asian sport) made of rattan, clay figurines, *wayang* (shadow puppet ► 112) figures and plenty more in Ubud's only toy shop.
✉ **Jalan Hanoman**
☎ **0361-975393**

Tattoo
This body-piercing studio has clean, sterilised equipment and offers a wide range of icons, patterns and pictures.
✉ **4 Jalan Hanoman**
☎ **0361-484833**

Fixed Prices
Shopping for souvenirs and gifts can prove a time-consuming process. Comparing prices, negotiating in one shop and then another shop ... it all takes time. The department stores in Kuta and Nusa Dua have fixed prices and you can browse without the sales chat. What you may lose by way of the price is often worth it in terms of time saved.

Beaches & Fun Parks

Children are Welcome

The Balinese are warmly affectionate and positive about children, and travellers should experience no problems taking them into restaurants or bars. Kuta now has its share of franchised fast-food places serving burgers and chips and, although children's menus are unusual, there is generally always something for them, chicken perhaps, on menus. All the better hotels have swimming pools and the upmarket resort hotels nearly all have a shallow pool for children.

Beaches

Kuta Beach

Every year there are tragic drownings off Kuta Beach because overambitious surfers and swimmers underestimate the power of the waves. However, if you stick to the designated areas between the flags there is no need to worry and children under supervision will enjoy the sea and sand. Kuta is home to Bali's biggest beach resort, with a strong Australian bias, and the white-sand beach stretches for 10km.

Sanur Beach

Many visitors consider Sanur beach to be the best on Bali. The shore stretches for about 4.5km but the best sand is to be found in the northern part near where the Grand Bali Beach hotel is situated. Older children will love the variety of water sports that are available, including windsurfing, parasailing, jet skiing and canoeing, and equipment may be hired on the beach or from most of the larger hotels that front the sea. With very young children, it is sometimes difficult to find shady places on the sand.

Snorkelling

Children, under the supervision of an accompanying adult in the water, will be enthralled by the experience of snorkelling, and the reefs surrounding Bali and Lombok offer superb opportunities. The inexperienced should begin by snorkelling off a beach area in shallow water. Worth considering for older children is a PADI certified diving course. There are diving centres in Kuta, Sanur, Lovina and Candi Dasa in Bali, and Senggigi in Lombok. A four-day course costs around Rp800,000 (or about US\$350).

✉ **Lovina and Candi Dasa in Bali and the Gili Islands off Lombok are the best places for inexperienced snorkellers.**

Fun Parks

Adrenalin Park

The young may prefer just to watch but older children may be tempted by The Slingshot which propels two passengers, in one capsule, over 50m in two seconds. If you are really unlucky they will be tempted to try the 50m bungee jump from a purpose-built tower. There is also an artificial rock face for climbing under the supervision of qualified instructors.

✉ **69 Benesari Street, Kuta**
☎ **0361-757841**

Waterbom Park

A recreational complex for all the family with water rides and swimming pools. Race tracks that begin at the top of a 16m tower and shoot riders down at speeds of up to 50km per hour (getting airborne for a moment or two!) will appeal to reckless youngsters. Positively relaxing by comparison are the jungle rides and the river rides in tube rafts. The slides appeal to younger children. Your own food and drinks need to be smuggled in, but there are restaurants inside.

✉ **Jalan Kartika Plaza, Tuban**
☎ **0361-755676**

Culture & Wildlife

Culture

Music
Children may enjoy sitting as close to a *gamelan* orchestra (➤ 112) as possible because this provides an opportunity to admire the skill of the musicians who perform at breathneck speed. Young children, on the other hand, may be disconcerted by being too close to the jangling noise of so many percussion instruments.

Shadow Puppet Drama
Children enjoy the novelty of a shadow puppet performance (*wayang kulit* ➤ 112), the pure skill of the one-man show and the surprising theatricality that a good puppet master can create. The narratives are usually drawn from Hindu epics so brush up on your knowledge of the *Ramayana* and *Mahabarata* epics. Performances usually take place at night after the sun has set. Ask at your hotel.

Traditional Dances
For children, some of the traditional dances are more suitable than others. The *legong* should be avoided because its refined style lacks the kind of drama that children respond to. The *Barong and Rangda* dance is basically an encounter between 'Good' and 'Evil' and the basic plot is easy to follow. Very young children may find the costume and appearance of the evil Rangda a little frightening if sitting too close to the stage. The *Sanghyang Jaran* dance is popularly advertised as the 'Fire Dance' and, as it features men dancing through a fire of coconut husks using a wooden hobbyhorse, it should engage the attention of children.

✉ **Dances are advertised everywhere in Kuta and Ubud and take place every night of the week**

Wildlife

Bali Barat, Taman Nasional
Once upon a time visitors would have seen tigers in the Bali Barat National Park. They are long gone, but there are long-tailed macaques, barking and sanbar deer, and the very rare Bali starling (➤ 13, 56).

Dolphin Trips from Lovina
An early morning start 6AM to see cavorting dolphins at play off the northern coast is easily arranged in Lovina. Travellers have conflicting opinions about the worth of this exercise but children should enjoy the spectacle.

✉ **All hotels around Lovina will arrange a trip**

Taman Burung
Bali Bird Park (Taman Burung) is home to over 150 species of birds, and over a thousand animals in all, some of which are seldom seen outside of Indonesia. Star attractions include resplendent birds of paradise from Irian Jaya and Komodo dragons. The 12m-high walk-in aviary is impressive and children may like the idea of breakfasting with the cockatoos or photo opportunities with some of the birds.

✉ **Jalan Serma Cok Ngurah Gambir, Singapadu (just north of Batubulan)** 🕐 **Daily 9–6** ☎ **0361-299352**

Babies
Disposable nappies are available in the supermarkets of Kuta and Sanur, as well as Ubud, but they cost more than at home. It helps to bring as many necessary items as possible in your luggage, especially wipes. Up-market hotels can generally arrange babysitters. Restaurants are happy to boil water for bottles, but it is best to always use bottled water. Remind youngsters never to drink tap water.

Traditional Dances & Music

Dances in Ubud

The very best place to enjoy an authentic dance performance is around Ubud (especially at Puri Saren Agung ➤ 55). There is a schedule with three or four different dances each night of the week and tickets can be purchased at the tourist office (☎ 0361-96285). Seats cannot be reserved so turn up early for a front-row view. Photography is allowed. Dances usually have a fixed admission rate but a transport charge is added if the venue is not within walking distance.

Dances

Different traditional dances take place regularly in southern Bali and in Ubud and at least one performance should be seen.

✉ **Ubud, Batubulan, Sanur, Nusa Dua, Denpasar. Tickets purchased in advance or at the door. Some restaurants include a dance performance before dinner.**

The Kecak

This 'monkey dance' is one of the more famous dances, its onomatopoeic name coming from the 'cak cak cak' chattering noise made by the chorus. The tale, from the *Ramayana*, tells of Rama and his monkey army attempting to rescue his wife from the clutches of the evil Rawana. The dance is dramatic, fast and musically arresting.

The Barong and Rangda

This dance enacts a struggle between the fun-loving Barong and the evil witch Rangda. It is one of the more enjoyable dances and usually includes a scene where the witch uses magic to force her adversaries to stab themselves with their own knives. The spell-binding costumes are invariably magnificent. In Ubud, the *calonarang* is an embroidered version of this dance with a witch queen, Calonarang, furious because no one will marry her daughter.

The Sanghyang Jaran

This trance dance tends to be advertised as the 'Fire Dance' because, in one version, participants dance over burning coconut husks.

The Legong

The *legong*, relatively lacking the narrative drama of the other dances, is highly refined and elegant. The kidnapped-princess-in-distress plot plays second fiddle to the courtly and intricate movements of the young girls who perform the dances.

The Baris

This is a warrior dance usually performed by men, either solo or in a small group, expressing the various emotions of the knightly combatant as he prepares for a battle.

Music

Gamelan Orchestra

The music is loud and brazen but also highly structured and requires speed of execution. Try to see the unique all-women orchestra in Ubud that performs every Sunday evening.

✉ **Jalan Puri Peliatan, Peliatan, Ubud**
☎ **0361-96285**

Shadow Puppet Drama

A *wayang kulit* (shadow puppet) performance consists of a small orchestra, up to 100 or more puppets and the *dalang* (puppet-master). The puppets are made from pieces of water-buffalo hide. Despite the language problem, a *wayang kulit* can be enjoyed and appreciated through the music and the incredible skill of the *dalang* in manipulating the puppets and adopting changes of voice.

✉ **Okra Kartini in Ubud**
☎ **0361-96285** 🕐 **Sun & Wed at 8PM**

Sports

Bali and Lombok

Scuba Diving
Bali and Lombok are inexpensive places to complete a certified diving course and gain a life-long PADI (Professional Association of Diving Instructors) certificate. The best diving sites are away from the busy tourist areas and require a boat trip to get there. Kuta, Sanur, Lovina and Candi Dasa in Bali all have well-established diving operators. Senggigi in Lombok and the Gili Islands also have operators. Some companies will be more professional than others so shop around and ask lots of questions.

Surfing
Bali is one of the world's surfing meccas and aficionados wax lyrical about the perfect 'tubes' (the space inside a breaking wave) they have experienced. All the necessary equipment can be bought in Kuta, or bring your own board, helmet and reef shoes. The best surfing spots are Kuta, Nusa Dua, Nusa Lembongan and, for the more experienced surfer, Uluwatu. Inexperienced surfers should strictly keep within the designated area on Kuta beach because there are regular fatalities, often caused by strong under-currents, when surfers head off on their own.

South and Southeast Bali

Bali International Rafting
This company organises adventure rafting trips down a 12km stretch of the River Telaga Waja, in the southeast of Bali, north of Klungkung. The rafting lasts about two hours and the package trip includes transport and lunch.
✉ 7 Jalan By Pass Ngurah Rai, Sanur ☎ 0361-281408

Bungee Jumping
There are at least four companies in Bali offering a leap of faith and a guaranteed rush of adrenalin. They can be relied on for professional equipment. The Bali Bungy Co (▶ 93) arranges free transport within the Kuta, Sanur and Nusa Dua area and a free T-shirt and certificate awaits those who live to tell the tale!
Bali Bungy Co ☎ 0361-752658/755425
Adrenalin Park ☎ 0361-757841

Sobek
Sobek is an adventure tour company specialising in white-water rafting trips on the River Ayung, jungle treks, sea-kayaking, bird-watching expeditions, and a spectacular descent of Gunung Batur on a bicycle.
✉ 9 Ian Tirta Ening, By Pass Ngurah Rai Sanur ☎ 0361-287059

Central and West Bali

Bali Adventure Tours
Well-organised kayaking, mountain cycling and jungle treks in addition to adventure rafting down the River Ayung. Package trips include transport, equipment, lunch, insurance and qualified instructors.
✉ Adventure House, Jalan By Pass Ngurah Rai, Pesanggaran or at Yanies restaurant (▶ 93) ☎ 0361-721480

Snorkelling
Bali and Lombok are both surrounded by reefs, which makes snorkelling one of the best forms of free entertainment on the islands. Bring your own gear or hire it on the beach at Sanur in southern Bali, Candi Dasa in southeastern Bali, Lovina in northern Bali, or the Gili Islands off Lombok.

Bars, Pubs & Nightclubs

Peanuts Pub Crawl
Book ahead for a place in Kuta's infamous and oversubscribed pub crawl. Every Tuesday and Saturday it starts at 6:30PM and a bus carts the increasingly inebriated group from one drinking hole to another. The opening venue is the Casablanca bar, then the two Peanuts bars, then...
☎ 0361-754149

South and Southeast Bali

Bukit Peninsula
Indian Ocean Cave Night
The Bali Cliff hotel (see The Ocean ➤ 92) organises a relatively expensive beach event on Wednesdays and Saturdays at 7PM, starting with cocktails and followed by a barbecue buffet and *Kecak* dance.
✉ Bali Cliff Hotel ☎ 0361-771992 (ext 890)

Candi Dasa
Candy Agung
At the west end of Candi Dasa, on the main road, this restaurant hosts a *Legong* dance to accompany the set three-course dinner each evening. The food is European and Balinese and the highly formalised *Legong* is an appropriate choice of dance for this context.
✉ Jalan Raya, Candi Dasa

Legend Rock Café
Live music on the stage each evening in a convivial pub atmosphere. Curries and pizzas served throughout the evening and an impressive drinks menu lists all the cocktails you can think of. Easy to find along the main road in Candi Dasa.
✉ Jalan Raya, Candi Dasa
☎ No phone

Kuta
The Bounty
Extraordinary building imitating Captain Bligh's ship, complemented by a full bar crew in naval uniforms. Happy hour is 6–8PM and 10PM–12AM with dancing from around 10PM. Leave by 2AM or walk the plank!
✉ Jalan Legian, Kuta ☎ 0361-752346

Casablanca Bar
There is a pool table, music and food in the Casablanca, a popular bar and meeting place. The infamous Peanuts Pub Crawl (see panel) takes over the place twice-weekly, but the atmosphere is always animated.
✉ 14 Jalan Buri Sari, Kuta
☎ 0361-751333

Hard Rock Café
This place, part of the famous international chain, is mercifully less self-important than some co-franchisees. There is no cover charge, no beefy bouncers, and there is a band performing live music from 11:15 each night. The place is too small for dancing but food is available, tacos and steaks mostly.
✉ 204 Jalan Legian, Kuta
☎ 0361-20451

Lips Bar
Anyone pining for country and western music will enjoy Lips Bar where the music lasts through the night until around 4AM the next morning. Food is available and on a Sunday there is often an acoustic guitar show from before noon until mid-afternoon.
✉ Legian Kuta Bali
☎ 0361-754630

Peanuts Club
One of the more popular nightclubs in Kuta. Air-conditioned with a large dance floor, DJ and music, pool tables and karaoke bar. Opens at 9PM; free entry before midnight.
✉ Corner of Jalan Melasti and Jalan Legian ☎ 0361-754149

Warung Tapas

A Spanish restaurant more noted for its live music and party atmosphere than its cuisine. The atmosphere really takes off around midnight. Telephone ahead to check that something is happening.

✉ **Jalan Raya Basangkasa, Seminyak, Kuta** ☎ **0361-751386**

Nusa Dua
Quinn's

Dance the night away with music from a live band or just sit and enjoy the scene in air-conditioned comfort.

✉ **Sheraton Laguna, Nusa Dua** ☎ **0361-71906**

Central and West Bali

Ubud
Café Arma

This Italian restaurant, delightfully situated in a rural setting, has live music various nights of the week (► 58).

✉ **Jalan Hanomen** ☎ **0361-975742**

Casa Luna

This pleasantly cultured restaurant (► 95) occasionally arranges evenings of live traditional music; check the pavement notice board.

✉ **Jalan Raya** ☎ **0361-96283** 🕐 **8–10**

Putra Bar & Restaurant

A wide-screen movie at 7PM followed by live music at 9PM for a two-hour performance. An inexpensive set three-course meal is available but not obligatory. The bar opens at 5PM.

✉ **Monkey Forest Road, Ubud** ☎ **0361-975570**

Saini Bar & Restaurant

A wide-screen movie is shown each evening at 7PM and after this a group of musicians will perform a jam session. This is as boisterous as it gets in sedate Ubud. The bar is easily found halfway down Monkey Forest Road, just past the playing fields.

✉ **Monkey Forest Road, Ubud** ☎ **0361-975570**

North and East Bali

Lovina
Malibu

Nightlife around Lovina is very low-key and there are no discos or nightclubs. A few restaurants, and especially the Malibu restaurant (► 98), organise evenings of live music. The restaurant at the Rambutan Beach Cottages (► 103) is also worth checking out for the occasional Balinese dance show accompanying dinner.

✉ **Kalibukbuk** ☎ **0362-41671** 🕐 **8–1**

Lombok

Senggigi
The Pub Downstairs

Nightlife in Lombok is restricted to the few bars in Senggigi and on Gili Trawangan. The Pub Downstairs, below the Princess of Lombok restaurant (► 99), has a pool table, darts and wide-screen video but that's about it. Occasionally, some of the other restaurants have an evening of live music or even a traditional Sasak dance.

✉ **Jalan Raya, Senggigi** ☎ **0370-93011**

Bars

The bars and pubs in Kuta are unlike anywhere else in Bali or Lombok. At their best they are lively and amusing and provide a good night's entertainment; at their worst, they are loud and rowdy and not to everyone's taste. In Ubud, by comparison, they are sedate and in Candi Dasa and Lovina they occasionally burst into life but are usually fairly tranquil establishments.

What's On When

Bamboo Poles and *Banten*

A sure sign of a festival or ceremony taking place in Bali are tall bamboo poles arching over the road leading into a village and brightly decorated with patterns made from the yellow leaf of coconut trees. Even more dramatic are the stunning pyramids of fruit and flowers – known as *banten* – that the women balance on their heads as they solemnly make their way to the village temple. The *banten* is an offering from the whole village to their gods and are often left overnight in the temple before being taken apart the next day.

Public Holidays

Only a few special days occur at the same time each year in Bali and Lombok and these include New Year's Day, Christmas Day and 17 August (Independence Day). The times of the most interesting holidays vary because they are calculated according to Balinese and Muslim lunar calendars.

Hindu New Year

The Hindu calendar calculates the beginning of the New Year (*Nyepi*) to be around the beginning of April or late March and the days before this are characterised by processions from temples and ceremonies to expel evil spirits. The night before *Nyepi* everyone bangs gongs, blows whistles and makes as much noise as possible to scare away the evil spirits for another year.

Muslim New Year and Ramadan

The Muslim New Year usually occurs in June or July although, from a Lombok visitor's point of view, the Ramadan month of fasting that takes place around late January and early February is more significant. Ramadan is the ninth month of the Muslim year, and strict fasting is observed from sunrise to sunset. Most restaurants outside of Senggigi will close between dawn and dusk.

Odalan Festivals

Every temple in Bali has its own *odalan* (birthday festival) and there will be other occasions that call for village festivities based around the temple. The highlight is usually the joyful afternoon procession of female villagers to the temple carrying their offerings. In the outer courtyard there will be a *gamelan* orchestra, dances perhaps or a shadow play (*wayang kulit* performance ▶ 112). Visitors are welcome to attend and unobtrusive photography is permitted. The Tourist Board issues a free calendar (see below) each year listing the dates of *odalan* festivals, which vary from year to year.

Finding a Festival

A comprehensive calendar of festivals and special events is available from government tourist offices in Kuta, Ubud or Singaraja, and the free tourist newspapers will also carry details of up-coming events. The tourist office in Ampenan, in Lombok, also issues a calendar of events covering Balinese and Sasak festivals and events around the island. If you stay for more than a week you should find an opportunity to observe and enjoy a Balinese festival, and it should prove to be a highlight of your visit.

Practical Matters

TIME DIFFERENCES

GMT 12 noon	Bali & Lombok 8PM	Germany 1PM	USA (NY) 7AM	Netherlands 1PM	Spain 1PM
	→	→	←	→	→

BEFORE YOU GO

WHAT YOU NEED

- ● Required
- ○ Suggested
- ▲ Not required

	UK	Germany	USA	Netherlands	Spain
Passport	●	●	●	●	●
Visa	▲	▲	▲	▲	▲
Onward or Return Ticket	●	●	●	●	●
Inoculations (Y fever, smallpox, typhoid, cholera, hepatitis A & B , malaria)	○	○	○	○	○
Health Documentation (▶ 123, Health)	○	○	○	○	○
Travel Insurance	○	○	○	○	○
Driving Licence (International)	●	●	●	●	●
Car Insurance Certificate (if own car)	●	●	●	●	●
Car Registration Document (if own car)	●	●	●	●	●

WHEN TO GO

Bali (coastal): highland temperatures may be cooler

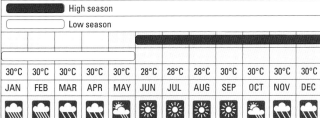

High season

Low season

JAN	FEB	MAR	APR	MAY	JUN	JUL	AUG	SEP	OCT	NOV	DEC
30°C	30°C	30°C	30°C	30°C	28°C	28°C	28°C	30°C	30°C	30°C	30°C

 Very wet   Wet   Sun   Sunshine & showers

TOURIST OFFICES

In the UK (for UK, Ireland, Benelux and Scandinavia)
Indonesia Tourist
Promotion Office,
3–4 Hanover Street,
London W1 9HH
☎ (0171) 493 0030
Fax: (0171) 493 1747

In the USA
Indonesia Tourist
Promotion Office,
3457 Wilshire Boulevard,
Los Angeles, CA90010
☎ 213/387 2078
Fax: 213/380 4876

In Germany (for rest of Europe)
Indonesia Tourist
Promotion Office,
Wiessenhutten Strasse, 17
D6000, Frankfurt-am-Main
☎ (069) 233677/233678

POLICE 110

FIRE 113

AMBULANCE 118

WHEN YOU ARE THERE

ARRIVING

The national airline, Garuda Indonesia, flies directly to Bali from Paris, Amsterdam and Vienna (in Europe) and Los Angeles (USA). Garuda Indonesia and other airlines also fly to Jakarta from where you transfer to a domestic flight for Bali or Lombok.

Ngurah Rai Airport, Bali
Km to centre of Denpasar

13 kilometres

Journey times	
	N/A
	20 minutes
	15 minutes

Selaparang Airport, Lombok
Km to centre of Senggigi

10 kilometres

Journey times	
	N/A
	30 minutes
	30 minutes

MONEY

The monetary unit of Bali and Lombok is the Indonesian rupiah (Rp). There are coins of 25, 50, 100 and 500 rupiah. Notes are in denominations of 100, 500, 1,000, 5,000, 10,000, 20,000 and 50,000 rupiah. It is an idea to carry smaller denominations (50 and 100 rupiah) as taxi drivers and small stores may not have small change. Travellers' cheques can be cashed at hotels, banks and money changers. Credit cards are widely accepted in popular tourist resorts on Bali.

TIME

 Bali and Lombok operate on Central Indonesia Standard Time, which is eight hours ahead of Greenwich Mean Time (GMT +8).

CUSTOMS

 YES

There are specific allowances of alcohol, cigarettes and luxury goods into the country for those over 16 years of age.

Alcohol:	2 litres
Cigarettes:	200
Cigars:	50 or
Tobacco:	100 grams
Perfume:	reasonable amount
Toilet water:	reasonable amount

Cameras and other photographic equipment (including video), radios and typewriters should be declared and recorded in your passport. These must be taken back out on your departure.

NO

Narcotics, guns and ammunition, TV sets, radio cassette recorders, Chinese medicines. The import or export of Indonesian currency exceeding 50,000 rupiah is prohibited.

CONSULATES

UK and Canada
have no consulates.
Use Australia/New
Zealand: 235093

Germany
288535

USA
288478

Netherlands
751517

France
233555

WHEN YOU ARE THERE

TOURIST OFFICES

Bali Government Tourism Office
● Jalan Surpati Parman
  Niti Mandala
  Renon, Denpasar
  ☎ (0361) 222387

Bali Government Tourism Office (Department of Tourism, Post and Telecommunications)
● Jalan Raya Puputan
  Niti Mandala
  Renon, Denpasar
  ☎ (0361) 225649

Badung (South Bali) Government Tourism Information Centre
● Jalan Bakung Sari
  Kuta, Denpasar
  ☎ (0361) 251419

Denpasar Government Tourism Office
● Jalan Surpati
  Denpasar
  ☎ (0361) 223602

Ngurah Rai Int Airport
● Tuban, Denpasar
  ☎ (0361) 51011

Kuta Art Market
● Jalan Bakung Sari
  Kuta, Denpasar

Bina Wisata Ubud
● Gianyar (next to village
  head's office of Ubud)

Lombok (West Nusa Tenggara Tourist Office)
● Jalan Langko 70
  Ampenan
  ☎ (0364) 21866

NATIONAL HOLIDAYS

J	F	M	A	M	J	J	A	S	O	N	D
(2)	(1)	(2)	(3)	1			2		1		1

1 Jan	New Year's Day
Jan/Feb	Chinese New Year
Mar/Apr	Balinese New Year (*Nyepi*)
Mar/Apr	Good Friday
21 Apr	Kartini Day
May	Ascension Day
15 Aug	Assumption Day
17 Aug	Independence Day (*Proklomasi Kemerdekaan*)
5 Oct	Armed Forces Day
25 Dec	Christmas Day

Other national holidays have dates that, being based on calendars other than the Western (Gregorian) calendar, change significantly every year. Check with a Balinese calendar during your visit.

OPENING HOURS

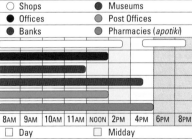

○ Shops	● Museums
● Offices	◐ Post Offices
● Banks	◐ Pharmacies (*apotiki*)

| 8AM | 9AM | 10AM | 11AM | NOON | 2PM | 4PM | 6PM | 8PM |

☐ Day	☐ Midday
☐ Evening	

In addition to the times in the chart, some shops do not close for lunch, but remain open through the day. Most shops are open Saturday and some also open Sunday. Offices close at 11AM Friday and 12.30PM Saturday. Banks close at 11AM Saturday and are shut Sunday. Banks in hotels open longer hours. Money changers are generally open until the evening.

Museum opening times vary (see individual museums in the 'What to See' section).

Most pharmacies open on Saturday. On Sundays they open on a rotation basis.

DRIVE ON THE
LEFT

TOILETS
FREE

There are very few public WCs. Tourist hotels have Western-style WCs. Elsewhere they are squat lavatories, take your own toilet roll.

PUBLIC TRANSPORT

Inter-island Flights There are regular daily flights between Bali (Denpasar) and Lombok (Mataram). Flight time is 25 minutes. Services are operated by Garuda-Merpati (Bali ☎ 0361 222864; Lombok ☎ 0370 32226) and Sempati (Bali ☎ 0361 288823; Lombok ☎ 0370 21612). There are also flights from Bali and Lombok to Sumbawa, a small island east of Lombok. The planes are quite small so book early.

Buses On Bali buses cover the main 'inter-town' routes, with Denpasar as the central terminal. In addition, all main routes, as well as minor passable ones, are covered by *bemos* (minibuses) – sometimes called 'colts' after the Mitsubishi Colt. On Lombok public buses and *bemos* cover the main routes. Off the main routes you may be restricted to a pony cart (*cidemo*).

Ferries There is a regular 24-hour car ferry service between Bali (Padangbai) and Lombok (Lembar). The trip takes at least four hours, sometimes up to seven hours. Alternatively, there is the faster, jet-powered catamaran, the *Mabua Express*, from Bali's Benoa Harbour to Lembar. The trip takes two hours but is more expensive than the ferry (information: Bali ☎ 0361 272370; Lombok ☎ 0370 81225).

Urban Transport In Denpasar, *bemos* (see Buses, above) skirt the central area, going between the various bus/*bemo* terminals and to other points around the city. In the city centre, three-wheeled mini-*bemos* (*tiga rodas*) are the main mode of transport; you find them lined up at each of the terminals (a letter on the back indicates their route). This is the main form of transport for other towns.

CAR RENTAL

On Bali local operators are cheaper than big international rental operators. An International Driving Permit is needed. On Lombok you arrange to borrow a private owner's car. You may need a licence and to leave your passport as security: check insurance cover.

TAXIS

Blue and yellow (air-conditioned) taxis are becoming more common in Denpasar and some tourist areas of Bali, but do not use one whose meter 'isn't working'. For taxis from the airport pay at the counter prior to your journey. Refuse offers from touts at the airport.

DRIVING

There is a two-lane motorway between Denpasar and Benoa.
Speed limit: **96 kph.**

Speed limit on all country roads: **96kph**

Speed limit on urban roads: **48kph**

Seat Belts
No laws at present.

Breath Testing
There are no laws, but avoid alcohol when driving.

Petrol (*bensin*) is sold by the government-owned Pertamina company and is reasonably cheap. You will find petrol stations in every large town, however in rural areas they are few and far between – when you see one, fill up. In an emergency there are roadside shops selling fuel from a drum, but this will be more expensive.

With the exception of the Denpasar–Benoa motorway, most roads are badly pot-holed or are tracks. Punctures are a common occurence; fortunately you will rarely be far from someone who can fix it for you (look for signs: 'Presban', 'Servis' or 'Bengkel'). Check your car for a spare tyre before driving it away. Contact the hire company for any other breakdown.

PERSONAL SAFETY

Crime against the person is rare in Bali and Lombok but you should guard belongings against theft. On Bali the Lake Batur area is crime-prone and the Kintamani-Bangli region is dubious. Items are rarely recovered.

To help prevent crime:

- Avoid walking after dark.
- Beware if you travel on local buses/*bemos*.
- Do not leave possessions unattended anywhere.
- Never carry your passport, airline ticket or more money than you need.
- Lombok is a Muslim island, exposing flesh is offensive.

Police assistance:
☎ **110**
from any call box

TELEPHONES

Bali and Lombok's telephone service is operated by Telekom. There are several types of public phone, some allow international calls and some take phone cards (*kartu telepon*). You can also use Telekom offices (*kantor telekomunikasi*), usually called *wartels*, where you pay at the desk at the end of your call.

International Dialling Codes

From Bali to:

UK:	101 44
Germany:	101 49
USA:	101 1
Netherlands:	101 31
Spain:	101 34

POST

Post Offices
Many hotels provide postal services, or there is a post office in every major town and village. In Denpasar the main post office is at Jalan Raya Puputan, Renon ☎ (0361) 223568.
On Lombok: Jalan Langko, Mataram.
Open: 8AM–2PM (8AM–noon Fri, 1PM Sat). Closed Sun.

ELECTRICITY

The power supply in most hotels is:
220 volts, 50 cycles AC (some districts still 110 volts).

 Sockets accept two-round-pin-style plugs.

Electrical appliances without dual voltage may require a voltage transformer.
For most Western visitors, an electrical adaptor is needed.

TIPS/GRATUITIES

Yes ✓ No ✗		
Tipping is not normal practice on Bali or Lombok. Do not insist on giving anyone a tip as many islanders look on tipping as charity and find it humiliating.		
Hotels (if service not included)	✓	10–15%
Restaurants (if service not included)	✓	10–15%
Bar service	✓	10%
Taxis (negotiate price first, tip optional)	✓	10–15%
Tour guides	✓	change
Porters	✓	Rp1,000
Hairdressers	✓	Rp1,000

PHOTOGRAPHY

What to photograph: Bali and Lombok are very photogenic islands. Most people do not object to being photographed but it is polite to ask. Never photograph in a public bathing place.

When to photograph: Shoot early in the day; it becomes hazy later and pictures may have a 'washed out' appearance.

Where to buy film: A good variety of film is widely available at reasonable prices, as is developing and printing, in innumerable photographic shops, chemists and stores.

HEALTH

Insurance

Medical insurance is essential, including provision to get 'medi-vacced' by air-ambulance if necessary. Specialist facilities are very limited but medical costs, therefore medical insurance, are not too expensive.

Dental Services

Have a thorough dental check-up before leaving home. It is not hard to find a dentist (*doktor gigi*) on Bali; in Denpasar there is Dr Indra Guizot, 19 Jalan Pattimura (☎ 0361 226455).

Sun Advice

Bali and Lombok are close to the Equator and the sun is immediately overhead all year round. It is easy to burn, even in the shade. Always wear a hat and sunglasses, drink plenty of fluids and wear a high-protection sunscreen.

Drugs

Most drugs, analgesics, antibiotics etc can be obtained at pharmacies (*apotik*) without prescription. Anti-malaria tablets should be taken before, during, and after your visit to Lombok (Bali is malaria-free). Take a small medical kit from home.

Safe Water

It is not safe to drink unboiled tap water. Good, bottled water (especially the 'Aqua' brand) is sold everywhere. Most ice is made with purified water but can be risky. Salads washed in local water are best avoided.

CONCESSIONS

Students/Youths: Bali and Lombok are ideal for youth travel. They offer bargain-priced adventure. Bali in particular is geared to young visitors and many find the surf, shops and bars in Kuta ideal. Your money will go further if you rent a room without air-conditioning, while you can get a cheap, filling meal from a *warung* (food stall). The International Student Identity Card (ISIC) is worth bringing as it is recognised by many places.

Senior Citizens: Bali and Lombok are not suitable for elderly tourists unless they are especially fit and can cope with the heat. The rough roads and temple stairways are very taxing.

CLOTHING SIZES

NB In Bali and Lombok
S = Small
M = Medium
L = Large

Bali and Lombok	UK	Rest of Europe	USA	
36	36	46	36	Suits
38	38	48	38	Suits
40	40	50	40	Suits
42	42	52	42	Suits
44	44	54	44	Suits
46	46	56	46	Suits
7	7	41	8	Shoes
7.5	7.5	42	8.5	Shoes
8.5	8.5	43	9.5	Shoes
9.5	9.5	44	10.5	Shoes
10.5	10.5	45	11.5	Shoes
11	11	46	12	Shoes
S	14.5	37	14.5	Shirts
S	15	38	15	Shirts
M	15.5	39/40	15.5	Shirts
M	16	41	16	Shirts
L	16.5	42	16.5	Shirts
L	17	43	17	Shirts
S	8	34	6	Dresses
S	10	36	8	Dresses
M	12	38	10	Dresses
M	14	40	12	Dresses
L	16	42	14	Dresses
L	18	44	16	Dresses
4.5	4.5	37.5	6	Shoes
5	5	38	6.5	Shoes
5.5	5.5	38.5	7	Shoes
6	6	39	7.5	Shoes
6.5	6.5	40	8	Shoes
7	7	41	8.5	Shoes

- There is an airport departure tax of Rp20,000 for international flights. Domestic airport travel tax is Rp7,000.
- Remaining Indonesian currency should be converted to a foreign currency before departure. There are facilities at Bali's airport.
- Reconfirm your flight between 24 and 72 hours before departure (vital in peak holiday periods).

WHEN DEPARTING

LANGUAGE

Bahasa Indonesia (literally 'Indonesia language') is the national language of Indonesia, but although widely used on Bali and Lombok, the local language is Balinese, or Bahasa Bali, which is altogether different with a different vocabulary. It is a very difficult language for a foreigner to get to grips with; for that reason it is best to use Bahasa Indonesia if you want to communicate with locals on Bali or Lombok. Indonesian is easy to learn as there are no tenses, no genders and often one word can convey the meaning of a whole sentence. In any case, many islanders speak English, particularly in major tourist centres.

Guesthouse, small hotel	*losmen*	soap	*sabun*
room	*kamar*	one night	*satu malam*
bed	*tempat tidur*	how much? (money)	*Berapa? (harga)*
toilet (WC)	*way say*	one person	*satu orang*
bathroom	*kamar mandi*	another, one more	*satu lagi*
boiled water	*air puti*	no/not/negative	*tidak/bukan*
		sleep	*tidur*

bank	*bank*	very	*sekali*
post office	*kantor pos*	expensive	*mahal*
How much?	*Berapa?*	one	*satu*
money	*harga*	two	*dua*
ticket	*karcis*	a half	*setenga, pronounced 'stenga'*

restaurant	*rumah makan*	rice	*nasi*
food	*makan*	potatoes	*kentang*
tea	*teh*	(fried/chips)	*(goreng)*
coffee (with milk)	*kopi (susu)*	vegetable salad	
beer	*bir*	(cooked)	*gado-gado*
water (drinking)	*air (minum)*	chicken	*ayam*
May we have our bill please?	*Coba berikan rekening saya?*	hot	*panas*
		cold	*dingin*
bread	*roti*	pineapple	*nanas*
fish	*ikan*	bananas	*pisanv*

bus	*bis*	I want to go to...	*Saya mau ke...*
ship	*kapal*	Where?	*Dimana?*
motorcycle	*sepeda motor*	Which way?	*Kemana?*
bicycle	*sepeda*	What time?	*Jam berapa?*
stop	*berhenti*	Where is..?	*Dimana ada..?*
village	*desa*	near	*dekat*

Good morning	*Selamat pagi*	Goodbye	*salamat tinggal*
Good day	*selamat siang*	Help!	*Tolong!*
no/not/negative	*tidak/bukan*	Call a doctor!	*Panggil dokter!*
Thank you	*terima kasih*	Call an ambulance	*Ambulin*
Please	*silakan*	My name is...	*Nama saya...*
sorry	*ma'af*	tomorrow/ yesterday	*besok/kemarin*
good, fine, OK	*baik*	I don't understand	*Saya tidak mengerti*

INDEX

Acknowledgements
The Automobile Association wishes to thank the following libraries, photographers and associations for their assistance in the preparation of this book:

KONINKLIJK INSTITUUT VOOR DE TROPEN 11b, 11c
MRI BANKERS' GUIDE TO FOREIGN CURRENCY 119
A J WALKER 122a, 122b
WORLD PICTURES F/cover a, c

The remaining pictures are from the Association's own library (**AA PHOTO LIBRARY**) and were taken by **JIM HOLMES** with the exception of the following:

D BUWALDA F/cover b, 2, 5a, 6b, 7b, 8c, 9c, 12a, 12/13, 14a, 16a, 16b, 17a, 18a, 19a, 18/19, 20a, 20b, 21a, 22a, 23a, 24a, 25a, 26a, 33b, 34b, 35b, 56, 60b, 61, 70b, 84, 86b, 91a, 91b, 92/116, 117b, 122c
B DAVIES 1, 8b, 9b, 10, 14b, 15a, 18b, 22b, 23b, 24b, 25b, 27b, 28/9, 36, 44b, 57, 63, 66, 77b, 78, 82, 85b, 87, 90b

Author's Acknowledgements
Sean Sheehan would like to thank the many kind people in Bali and Lombok who assisted him with the research of this book.

Contributors
Page Layout: Design 23 Verifier: Polly Phillimore
Researchers (Practical Matters): Colin Follett and Lesley Allard Indexer: Marie Lorimer

Dear Essential Traveller

**Your comments, opinions and recommendations are very
important to us. So please help us to improve our travel
guides by taking a few minutes to complete this simple
questionnaire.**

*You do not need a stamp (unless posted outside the UK). If you do not want to cut this page
from your guide, then photocopy it or write your answers on a plain sheet of paper.*

Send to: **The Editor, AA World Travel Guides,
FREEPOST SCE 4598, Basingstoke RG21 4GY.**

Your recommendations...

We always encourage readers' recommendations for restaurants, nightlife
or shopping – if your recommendation is used in the next edition of the
guide, we will send you a *FREE* AA *Essential* **Guide** of your choice.
Please state below the establishment name, location and your reasons
for recommending it.

_____
_____
_____
_____

Please send me **AA *Essential*** _____
(*see list of titles inside the front cover*)

About this guide...

Which title did you buy?
    AA *Essential* _____
Where did you buy it? _____
When? _ _ / _ _

Why did you choose an AA *Essential* Guide? _____
_____
_____
_____
_____

Did this guide meet your expectations?
    Exceeded ☐   Met all ☐   Met most ☐   Fell below ☐
    Please give your reasons _____
_____
_____
_____

continued on next page...

Were there any aspects of this guide that you particularly liked? _____
_____
_____
_____

Is there anything we could have done better? _____
_____
_____
_____
_____

About you…

Name (*Mr/Mrs/Ms*) _____
Address _____
_____
_____ Postcode _____
Daytime tel nos _____

Which age group are you in?
Under 25 ☐ 25–34 ☐ 35–44 ☐ 45–54 ☐ 55–64 ☐ 65+ ☐

How many trips do you make a year?
Less than one ☐ One ☐ Two ☐ Three or more ☐

Are you an AA member? Yes ☐ No ☐

About your trip…

When did you book? mm / y y   When did you travel? mm / y y
How long did you stay? _____
Was it for business or leisure? _____
Did you buy any other travel guides for your trip?
If yes, which ones? _____
_____

Thank you for taking the time to complete this questionnaire. Please send
it to us as soon as possible, and remember, you do not need a stamp
(*unless posted outside the UK*).

Happy Holidays!